When My Mind Wanders It Brings Back Souvenirs

by

Gordon Kirkland

authorHOUSE™

1663 LIBERTY DRIVE, SUITE 200
BLOOMINGTON, INDIANA 47403
(800) 839-8640
WWW.AUTHORHOUSE.COM

First published by AuthorHouse 04/28/05

ISBN: 1-4208-1149-5 (sc)
ISBN: 1-4208-1150-9 (dj)

Library of Congress Control Number: 2004099369

Printed in the United States of America
Bloomington, Indiana

This book is printed on acid-free paper.

In memory of my parents,

Vera Kirkland

who would be so proud

and C.A. (Bert) Kirkland

who would be so surprised

Also By Gordon Kirkland

<u>Books</u>
Justice Is Blind - And Her Dog Just Peed In My Cornflakes

Never Stand Behind A Loaded Horse

<u>Compact Disks</u>

Comedy
I'm Big For My Age

Audiobooks
Never Stand Behind A Loaded Horse - Live

The Gordon Kirkland Writer To Writer Series Compact Disks
Live At The Florida First Coast Writers' Festival - Write For Your Life

Writing Humor - Even On Days When You Don't Feel Funny

Table of Contents

Acknowledgements

As always these stories would not get written without the love and support of family and friends, many of whom can find themselves within these pages.

People often ask me what my wife thinks about appearing in so many of my stories. Diane likes to think that she has first right of veto of anything I might write, and I'll just keep letting her think that way. In fact, I could not be doing this without her support. It was Diane who encouraged me to start writing these stories. That led to the start of my newspaper column in 1994. It is Diane who keeps me going with her love and encouragement.

Our sons, Mike and Brad, have also been regular features in the stories. I know that they have been happy that the newspaper column does not appear in a local paper where their friends, and more importantly girlfriends' parents, might read about them. They, too, have been encouraging throughout the entire time I have been writing.

Of course there is also Tara, my disability assistance dog, who helps me walk. She is always there to let me know that no matter what I write, she thinks I am brilliant. She also makes sure that I take time to stop and smell the dog biscuits as often as possible every day.

My life has been filled with laughter from the very beginning, thanks largely to my brother Jim and my sister Lois. Together we laughed at and with each other, and found ways to 'put the f-u-n in dysfunctional' whenever and wherever possible. Anyone who feels sorry for my wife should feel equally sorry for Jim's wife, Carolyn and Lois' husband, Bob.

I also must acknowledge the support that so many friends have given me over the years including Wayne and Peggy Turner, Lars and Jan Gronmyr, and Blaine and Bretta Beveridge. I'm also very lucky to have good friends who share this crazy business and who encourage me to be a better writer by their examples, including Lynn Johnston, Ridley Pearson, and Bruce Cameron.

A special thanks to all the folks at AuthorHouse™, especially Michael Johnson, Kelly Barrow, Matt Power and Trina Lee, who helped make this book a reality.

Section One:
Commitment, Love, Marriage, and All That Other Flowery Stuff

If Creative Insanity Is An Art, I'm An Old Master

My wife often stares at me with deer-in-the-headlight looks and asks me to remind her again about whether or not she had a good reason to have married me nearly thirty-one years ago.

She claims that she wasn't informed that I was crazy, at the time.

Personally, I think my tenuous grasp on reality is one of my more charming attributes.

After over a quarter century of marriage most wives have gotten pretty used to the way their husbands behave. I'd be afraid that might get boring. Diane will never get used to the way I behave. She'll never know just what to expect next.

Quite frankly, I am never sure myself.

I'm not suggesting that I am prone do doing things that might give my wife a legal excuse to have me committed. I might push the envelope from time to time, but even I have my limits.

For example, I might walk naked into the bedroom from the bathroom, talking into an imaginary communicator saying, "OK, Scotty, I like a good joke as much as the next guy, but beam me down my clothes now!"

Eccentric…? Well, maybe a little, but it's still not something she could have me committed for.

Now if I was to walk into the living room doing the same thing when her boss is over for a visit, that might be different.

I'm a pretty curious person when it comes to looking for new experiences. That curiosity gives Diane an excuse to bring out the aforementioned deer-in-the-headlights look on a fairly frequent basis. The other day we needed to use her car on an errand.

I don't often get to enjoy the experience of sitting in the passenger seat. It was a nice day. The car windows were open. I started to think about how the dog behaves when she is in the car with her window open.

I decided to see what it felt like to stick my head out the window and let the wind make my cheeks flap. Diane obviously thought I had finally, once and for all, lost my mind.

Sure it was a bit on the unusual side, even for me, but I contend that it is a long way from insanity. If I had stuck my other cheeks out the window to see what it felt like to have them flap in the wind, I might agree that the time had come to have me fitted for a custom made straightjacket.

I try to employ one of my favorite eccentricities whenever I am taking money from a busy automated teller machine. When the money comes out of the machine I grab it, hold it over my head and shout, "I won! I won!"

I have a very good reason for doing this. We've all heard about people being robbed after making a withdrawal from one of those machines. I figure that any robber in his right mind would be afraid to try to mug somebody who is so crazy he thinks he hit a slot machine jackpot from a bank machine.

There is another side benefit to my behavior. Seeing the stunned looks on the faces of the other customers, the bank employees, and the armored truck deliverymen is just pure entertainment.

I have a tendency to respond to people's questions in ways that are technically correct answers, but just not the sort of answer they were expecting. An example of this occurred recently when I stopped at a gas station in Kentucky to get a cold drink and a snack for the road.

The cashier looked up from his book, glanced at my small purchase, and asked, "You got gas?"

"No," I replied, "just a little heartburn."

He was able to do the deer-in-the-headlights look almost as well as my wife.

Sparks Still Fly

My wife and I have been married for more than thirty years. After so many anniversaries, it's almost surprising that there are still a lot of sparks in the marriage.

Most of them involve static electricity.

Almost everyone experiences the occasional spark of static electricity, usually in dry cold weather. When we were kids it was considered great fun to slide our wool-socked feet on the carpet to build up a charge and then zap an unsuspecting sibling. In my family it may have been the major cause of my sister's incredibly straight hair.

Around here sparks of static electricity can be heard no matter what the weather. It can be hot and humid and I will still hear a crackle followed by my wife's scream. You might find it hard to believe, but I am not even involved in the shocking.

She does it all on her own.

Diane is so full of electricity that she could probably light and heat a small town. I'm thinking of suggesting that she stand in the corner of the living room with a light bulb in her hand, rather than spend the money on a new lamp. If we're ever faced with a lengthy power outage she could just hold onto the freezer's plug and save our frozen food from melting. Truth be told, she could probably jump-start a 1952 Mercury that's sat unused in a barn since 1959.

It's only been in the last year or so that she's been exhibiting her electrical generating powers. I'd hate to think what might have happened if she was like this earlier in our marriage and she tried to change one of our sons' wet diapers. The kid could have grown up with hair like Don King.

It comforts me to know that, should the situation ever arise, she could probably restart my heart without the need of a defibrillator. Whether she would or not seems to be in question.

Obviously there are some drawbacks to being married to an electrical generator. I really don't want her refueling the car whenever I am within a hundred yards of it. On the plus side, she could probably light the gas barbecue if she wasn't terrified of the thing.

The dog no longer brings her cold wet nose anywhere near Diane.

She even seems to defy the laws of physics with her electrical outbursts. One of the most frequent recipients of her static charges is our car. The car is sitting on rubber tires and should therefore be grounded. Virtually every time she gets out of the car and grabs onto the door to close it, she yelps and there is a slight scent of ozone and burning flesh in the air. She sparks in leather-soled shoes and she zaps in rubber-soled shoes. She crackles in wool, and she pops in cotton.

I've been wondering if I rubbed the cat against her, could she - and/or it - then be stuck to the wall like a charged balloon?

Diane belongs to one of those service clubs that requires its members to shake hands with everyone else in the room before the start of the meeting. Her handshakes are often greeted with a surprised, wide-eyed look. A few of the older incontinent members are afraid to go near her these days.

Television has shown several examples of this kind of behavior, but I can't get a clear answer to what is causing it. Watching programs last week would seem to indicate that:

1) She is a witch who chases demons;
2) She is a demon who chases witches;
3) She is a mutant with yet untapped powers;
4) She was abducted by aliens; or,
5) She is an alien.

None of these options sound all that appealing, and you'd think that after thirty years of marriage I would have noticed some other behavior that could be tied to one of those possibilities. Just be on the safe side though, I've started carrying a clove of garlic in my pocket.

I suppose on the greater scheme of things it isn't a very important issue. Diane has put up with a lot of odd behavior from me over the last thirty years. I guess I shouldn't complain about the odd jolt of electricity coming from her side of the bed.

To be honest, it's kind of nice to know that, even after so many years, there's still some sizzle in her.

Is That An Alien Probe, Or Are You Just Happy To See Me?

I'm not sure, but I think aliens may have abducted me a few days ago. The fact that I'm not sure just adds credibility to my assertion, because the most common symptom of people who claim to have been abducted by aliens is that they can't remember anything about it.

My wife and I were out for a drive and crossed the border into Washington State. On our way home we decided to stop by a lake that, according to the official state road map, was just to the east of Interstate 5. We took the appropriate off ramp. We headed east. After a mile or so the road turned to the north, just as the map indicated it would.

We never did find the lake. Even though it was clearly supposed to be where I thought we were, I wasn't about to bring my manhood into question by stopping to ask directions.

After what seemed like a short time, we found ourselves approaching Interstate 5. The map didn't say we'd do that. We hadn't turned off the original road at any point along our route. It was a bit disconcerting when we realized that we were approaching the interstate from the west, when we knew we had turned east when we left it. Not only that, we discovered that we were nearly fifteen miles further south than the spot we had turned off. The last turn either of us could remember was when the road curved north.

To make matters worse, nearly 45 minutes had elapsed.

Neither Diane nor I can remember turning south or west. We can't even remember crossing the interstate, but the evidence was against us. Somehow, we had arrived at that spot, and it defied any logical explanation how we had gotten there.

That's when I turned to illogical explanations.

The alien abduction theory seems like a good one, although I can't seem to find any evidence that alien probes have inspected my personal and intimate nooks and crannies. If they did, there don't seem to be any homing devices left in the usually reported places. We don't even have tags in our ears to indicate to future abductors that we have already been caught and released.

Wouldn't that be just my dumb luck? Aliens who are sloppy about their specimen handling practices abducted me. You would think these things would have some rules about putting their samples of humanity back facing the same direction as when they found them.

As we drove home, passing the same landmarks along the interstate that we had seen earlier, Diane said something that has me quite concerned. "How does that make you feel," she asked, "realizing that you've been abducted by aliens and they sent you back?"

Actually, I'm pretty glad they sent me back. I'm not all that crazy about flying in an airliner. I don't think I'm emotionally prepared for interstellar flight. It doesn't bother me to think that I might not have met the quality control standards of an alien race. What has me staring at the ceiling throughout the night is that Diane said, 'they sent you back,' not 'they sent us back."

What if they kept her and sent back an exact replica?

Oh sure, lots of husbands periodically think their wives are from another planet. Periodically they give us some pretty strong evidence that they are. Still, that little slip of the tongue has me really concerned. I'm starting to notice some irregularities that might otherwise just be chalked up to the normal inconsistencies of living with a woman.

For example, just last night, Diane watched a TV comedy that I like. That might not seem all that unusual, but this particular show is one that she really, really, really doesn't like. I don't think she's ever seen more that the opening credits before. Not only did she watch the show, but she also laughed uproariously at it. Diane and I have been married for 32 years. In all that time, I've learned what she does - and does not- find funny. That show is definitely in the 'does not' column, but there she was, whoever she was, laughing at it.

You can see why it has me a bit spooked.

For all I know, my wife is up there pointing out to some alien replica of me that the space ship could use a good dusting, and that she shouldn't be the only one who notices things like that.

If the aliens are as bad at putting the laundry in the laundry basket as they are at putting people back on the east side of the interstate facing north, I'm sure they'll be bringing her back in no time.

Rolling Stones May Break Her Bones

Over the years I've done a pretty good job of testing the resilience, or perhaps I should say lack of resilience, of my skeletal structure. I've broken a leg, an arm, my spine, more ribs than you'd find at a Chinese food buffet, and, perhaps most spectacularly, my right big toe.

I broke my arm falling off my bike when I was eight years old. Less than three weeks after the cast was removed I broke my leg playing a game at school. My mother didn't believe me when I told her that I was sure my leg was broken. She assumed that, after breaking the arm, I would think I broke something every time I hurt myself. Even my sister accused me of faking it to get attention. Finally, after four days of not being able to walk, my mother gave in and convinced my father to take me to the hospital. Dad's biggest concern, in those days before socialized medical care came to Canada, was not with my swollen leg. His conversation focused on what the eventual cost would be for x-rays and whatever else I might need.

I was almost glad when it turned out that the leg was indeed broken, because it sure added up to a whole mess of guilty feelings on my mother's part. She applied her guilty feelings just where I wanted them -- in the kitchen with an unending supply of cookies and other treats. I think I'm probably still carrying around several thousand fat cells that developed during those days.

My brother and sister were less gracious in their sympathy. Having my leg in a cast meant that I got to have one whole side of the dinner table to myself, while they shared the other side. They also had to put up with a stool between them for me to rest my leg on during dinner. Their feelings translated into a nightly ritual of "accidentally" pushing my leg off the stool and enjoying my reactions to the sudden leg jolt.

Despite these bits of sibling cruelty, my brother and I were, and remain, very close. When I was twelve I had a growth spurt that shot me several inches taller than my much, much older brother. I figured that it was time to show Jim just who the big brother really was. We had a disagreement over something that neither of us can remember. Neither of us will ever forget the result of that disagreement though. I ended up with a broken toe.

I broke it on Jim.

More accurately, I broke it on Jim's crotch.

It may well be the reason he fathered only daughters, while I fathered sons.

A few years ago, after I broke my spine, my sons went through their own period of bone breaking. At one point I was in my wheelchair, Mike had a cast on his leg, and Brad had a cast on his arm. Their mother was embarrassed to be seen in public with us, because wherever we went heads would turn, conversations would stop, and people would look at Diane wondering what she was doing to the rest of us.

Well, now it's her turn.

Last weekend we decided to put our house on the market. I guess we hadn't had enough stress in our lives for a while, so we needed something to raise our blood pressures. The sign barely had time to settle into the ground when disaster struck.

Naturally, like all couples trying to sell a house, we went into full-fledged clean-up mode to get it ready for prospective buyers. Part of that involved a considerable amount of yard work.

Diane always focuses a lot of attention on whatever she is doing. In this case she focused on getting the lawn done, which meant she was unable to focus on a rock that had somehow made its way into the carport. As she was taking the lawn mower out, she stepped on the rock. It rolled. Her foot rolled with it. One of the bones in her foot did not stand up to the rigors of rock and roll. As a result, it's difficult for her to stand up at all.

After years of being the one to maneuver around on crutches, it's interesting to see Diane try to do it. Amazingly, it isn't as easy as she thought it looked. She's just about reached the point where she can get around on the crutches with all the grace and agility of a wounded musk ox.

Naturally, I'm doing my best to appear sympathetic. At least I haven't laughed nearly as much as she did when I tried walking right after a vasectomy.

She's Outta There

Being the writer-in-residence at our house means that I am often called upon to assist other family members with writing tasks. This might take the form of proofreading a school assignment, editing a resume, or just putting together a grocery list.

Hey, we all have to be good at something...

This week, my writing skills were called upon for a very important document. After twelve years with the same company, my wife is about to make a career change. Therefore it's time to put together a letter of resignation.

I hate writing things like that. The person receiving it never has any true appreciation for the degree of creative thought that has gone into crafting just the right collection of nouns, verbs and adjectives that make up a finely tuned letter of this type. On the other hand, the person who wants me to write the letter never really wants me to let loose with all of my creative juices on her unsuspecting, and soon to be former, boss.

Something about not wanting to burn any bridges, yadda, yadda, yadda...

Still, I have to get all of the possibilities out of my system before I can stop thinking about what I could have written. For example, one thought was to put her letter into the style of the late Dr. Suess - something along the lines of, "The time has come. The time is now. Diane M. Kirkland is going to quit now. She's tired of you. She's got to leave. She's thinking thoughts you won't believe."

I considered using a fictional approach, perhaps something in the style of a mystery novel. "It was a dark and stormy morning, when [insert her boss's name here] entered the office and found a note fastened to his Corinthian leather chair with a menacing dagger. The words were clipped from the pages of newspapers and magazines and hastily glued to the paper. We have Diane Kirkland. We are holding her captive with more money and better benefits. You'll never see her again."

Of course the country and western approach crossed my mind. I could have simply recorded Johnny Paycheck's classic *Take*

This Job And Shove It, and given it to Diane to send to him in an email.

Every job has it own share of unique frustrations. Some of them are constant, while others come and go, seemingly at the whim of someone 'at head office.'

As husbands everywhere know only to well, when a wife is frustrated, EVERYBODY is frustrated.

Diane's frustrations at work played a major role in her decision to seek out a new employer. Listening to those frustrations on a daily basis played a major role in my unending support of her decision to seek out a new employer.

One of the most recent thorns in her side was the decision by head office to tell all of its employees that family pictures were no longer welcome in the office. It seemed like the sort of thing that cried out to be included in a letter of resignation,

I could have said something like, "Since I am no longer allowed to have a picture of my husband in the office, I have been forced to resort to imagining what he might be doing while I'm here at work. The picture only made me think of his face. Imagining the entire image also conjured up thoughts about the mess he might be making at home. This made it impossible for me to concentrate on my job. I have therefore taken a job with a company that will allow me to go back to just looking at his picture every now and again."

I even suggested a direct, to the point, no holds barred, burn the bridges, insulting approach along the lines of, "Dear Crap For Brains: I would like to say that it has been a pleasure to work for you these past many months since they promoted you beyond your capabilities to the position of manager of my area, but my mother always told me not to lie. Since you are clearly up the creek without an intellectual paddle, I have decided to get out while the getting is good. I'd hope you fry in hell, but you are so stupid you'd probably enjoy it because it's a dry heat."

Diane vetoed each and every one of those ideas. She wanted a bland letter that just gave the facts of the matter. She's taking a better opportunity, and she doesn't blame her boss for her decision. Naturally, I helped her put that kind of a letter together.

...but I didn't enjoy it one bit.

They Want What?

That age old question we all ask every so often never seems to get a satisfactory answer.

Men wonder just what it is that women want, and as long as they still have two or three functioning brain cells most men know better than to wonder about it out loud.

Women, on the other hand, wonder out loud about the great mystery of what men want, but in truth they know exactly what it is, they're just smart enough not to admit it in mixed company. They want men to be intuitive, but they also want to keep us as confused as possible.

OK. It's working. We're confused.

Forget the complicated needs and desires about love, security, and control of the thermostat. We have enough trouble understanding the simple things that women want.

Take laundry hampers for example. I have often said that my ability to hit the laundry hamper on a consistent basis is reduced due to a severe eye problem called retinal simplification. My eyes see that it is easier to hit the bedroom floor than the laundry hamper.

Still, I can understand that my wife would prefer to see my dirty socks neatly deposited in the hamper. In the past I've tried walking my dirty clothes right to the hamper and throwing them in. That's when I found out that she really doesn't want my dirty laundry in the hamper after all. Apparently she'd much prefer that I skip the laundry hamper all together. I should know that if I can put the laundry in the hamper, I can also be expected to put the whole mess in the washing machine instead.

Who knew?

I'm adaptable. I can accept that the laundry hamper is a place for pre-worn women's wear and mine are supposed to go directly into the washing machine. But that's still not what is really wanted. Apparently, I'm supposed to take her clothes out of the laundry hamper and add them to mine in the washing machine.

If that's all it takes to make her happy, I'll do it.

Apparently that's still not what it takes to make a woman happy. Leaving a washing machine full of dirty clothes does not do it for them. Get this: We're supposed to add detergent and turn the machine on too.

If you think that's the end of it, you're dumber than I am. Apparently women do not want wet laundry to sit in the washing machine for days at a time. They also want it to be put into the clothes dryer.

Sounds simple doesn't it?

Guess again.

Putting clothes in the dryer is much more complicated than reaching into the washing machine, pulling out whatever is in there and stuffing it all into the dryer. Some women's clothes don't go in the dryer. We're supposed to know the difference.

I already know that pantyhose don't go into the dryer. They are supposed to hang from the shower curtain rod looking like a herd of pythons about to jump on a bleary-eyed husband who gets up and goes into the bathroom in the middle of the night without fully regaining consciousness.

Apparently there are all sorts of clothes that don't go into the dryer. None of them are men's, mind you, but women actually expect us to read those hieroglyphics on clothing tags. That's just a bit too much like asking for directions when we're lost, or actually reading an instruction manual before assembling a bicycle. It's just not in our genetic makeup.

Even if we manage to get the dryer contents correct and remember to turn it on, we can still quite easily miss the mark about what women want. Hell hath no fury like a woman who gets out of the shower and discovers that her husband didn't add a fabric softener sheet to the dryer load with the towels. Guys are happy with towels that dry us off after our showers. We'd dry with sandpaper if we thought it would get us out the door faster. Women want to be dried, but with something soft and fluffy.

You'd think it would end there. A man can still be a major disappointment if he gets everything right to that point but doesn't take the clothes out of the dryer, fold them neatly, and put them away sometime that same week.

If we can't understand the importance they put on remembering fabric softener every single time, how can we be expected to understand why they wake us up in the middle of the night to ask "Is it really hot in here or is it just me?"

I may not really know what women want, but I am pretty sure it has something to do with making men as confused and bewildered as humanly possible.

That, and towels that don't scratch.

The Long and Costly Road

It may surprise some people to hear that my thirty-somethingth wedding anniversary is just a few days away. Probably the biggest surprise for most of you is that I have remembered that my anniversary is just a few days away.

Anyone who watches TV shows about family life will probably be surprised that a husband is actually remembers his anniversary. Based on what I have learned from watching these shows, husbands should not be capable of remembering to wash colors and whites in separate loads, successfully pick up the groceries without having the list tattooed onto the back of their hands, or naming the date of their wedding anniversary.

I learned that rule about the colors and whites in the laundry early in my married life. The other guys in the changing room at the pool only need to see you putting on bright pink boxer shorts once before that rule is etched indelibly in your brain.

I've always been reasonably successful at picking up what I need to at the grocery store. In fact I usually come home with more than I intend to because those ladies at the sample tables can be so intimidating.

I don't have to put a lot of effort into remembering that my anniversary is approaching. As soon as I see the back to school ads, I know it's fast approaching. In 1973 I prepared for my return to school by buying my textbooks, picking up loose-leaf paper, and getting married.

Diane and I had already decided to get married, and were encouraged to speed things up a bit by a nice little surprise. Some of you might think that means we were expecting a little bundle, and you wouldn't be entirely wrong. We just weren't expecting that kind of bundle. We discovered that we qualified for nearly three times the amount of money from the student loan program if we were married compared with what we would have gotten as singles.

Even with that great influx of capital, we were still slightly below the economic standards of the average church mouse. We didn't have a car. Our apartment was so small that even if we had the inclination - or if animals were allowed in the building -

we couldn't have swung a cat without hitting all four walls. Our version of a five-star restaurant had golden arches outside the building.

Looking back, we probably had more fun that first year than in many of the years when our economic situation was better.

As each year passes many people wonder how we have managed to stay successfully married for so many years when the divorce statistics are so high. Actually, what most people wonder is how Diane has put up with me for so many years. Some days I wonder about that too. I've often referred to Diane as "my first wife." She, in turn, calls me her "last husband." At least, that's what she calls me when she isn't wondering about the possibility of trading me in for two twenty-five-year-olds. I don't think she has much hope of that, because I've never seen a push-pull-drag sale for pre-owned husbands.

Having children was a major influence on the longevity of our marriage. It didn't take us too long to come to the conclusion that if we didn't stick together, the kids would outnumber whichever one of us got sentenced to single parenthood.

Safety in numbers isn't just for military forces.

Being a parent was hard enough with an ally. I'd hate to think what it would have been like if either of us had to do it on our own. Now that the boys are grown, we'd still like to avoid feeling outnumbered by our offspring.

On the other side of the coin they are both afraid that if anything did ever happen to break up their parents, one of them would end up with custody of me.

Diane asked me the other day if I had any ideas about how we should celebrate our anniversary this year. In years gone by we have slipped away for a private weekend, or at the very least, gone out for a dinner at a restaurant without golden arches. Looking back over the past years and thinking about just how much money it has cost us to get from the point where we were poorer than church mice to the point where we are now almost on a par with the average church mouse, I think there is really only one way to celebrate.

Cheese and crackers.

Vertical Dimension Is One Of My Wife's Shortcomings

My wife is at a severe disadvantage around here.

I realize that many of my readers might think that she is indeed disadvantaged having to be married to someone like me, but that's not the problem I'm talking about. Oh sure that might be a big disadvantage, but it's her vertical deficiency that seems to be causing the most problems for her.

Diane claims to be five-foot-four. As one of my sons says, "OK, Mom you can be 5'4", and I guess that makes me 7'2"."

I like to think of it another way. Diane can be just as tall as she wants to be as long as I can continue to say I weigh the same as I did in 1973.

Even if Diane is the height she claims to be, she's still at a serious disadvantage. She is constantly complaining that everything is designed for people who are not five-foot-four. I try to tell her that if things were designed for people her height, the rest of us would go around bumping our heads everywhere.

She thinks that's just the price we should have to pay for being taller.

Kitchen cupboards are one of her biggest stumbling blocks. As long as anything she wants is on the bottom shelf, or right at the front of the second shelf, she might be able to reach it. Above that, it might as well be in another dimension.

I don't think Diane has ever seen the top of a refrigerator, much less the things that get pushed to the back on our bedroom closet shelves.

She gets particularly perturbed when she discovers that we have gone to a restaurant and her feet can't touch the floor of the booth. It's surprising just how often this occurs, despite her claims that she is of average height. One would think that the average person could always place their feet flat on the floor from any chair.

It probably wouldn't bother her all that much if at least one of our sons had been born with her diminutive genes instead of my elongated ones. Both of our sons are over six feet tall, and I am just under six-foot four. It must be like constantly being the Lilliputian with a bunch of Gullivers. Shelves, refrigerator tops and restaurant chairs don't pose a problem for rest of us in the family.

I suppose we could be a bit more understanding of the problems faced by someone of Diane's height. For one thing we could try not laughing when she tries to reach things that are just slightly above our eyelevel.

It's not like being tall is any walk in the park either. I have been over six-foot since I was twelve years old. My tallest sibling is five-foot-nine. My father was shorter than that and my mother might have been five-foot if she stood on top of the dog.

No, I'm not sure how tall our milkman was in 1953.

As a teenager I had to put up with a low hanging light fixture right outside my bedroom door. Many were the mornings that I stumbled sleepily out of my room and cracked my head on the thing. It did allow me to be a good son. A good son gives his mother enjoyment, and when I would hit the light fixture my mother would get so much enjoyment she would often have to sit down for a few minutes to catch her breath.

At least Diane can walk through a store without worrying about being knocked unconscious by a low hanging sign announcing that oranges are only fifty-nine cents a pound this week. She doesn't have to be nervous around ceiling fans. She'll only know the pain that can result from a low tree branch if she's on horseback. She will never have to discover the hard way that the people who make portable outhouses make the doors too short.

Believe me; regaining consciousness on the floor of an outdoor privy is not nearly as pleasant as it sounds.

Diane will never have to put up with one of the great annoyances faced by those of us who are of superior height. No one will ever ask her "How's the weather up there?"

Our height difference hasn't really caused us that much of a disagreement over the thirty some years that we've been married. As the good and loving husband that I am, I have found that it is my place to do the compromising. I learned early that if I want to see eye-to-eye with her on anything I either have to sit down, or get her a stepladder.

Need A Vacation Planner?
Don't Call Me.

It seemed like the sort of thing that even I could get right.

When Diane's birthday came along a couple of months ago she said that she's like to go out on the water somewhere. I searched the Internet for ideas and came up with the San Juan Islands, just off the coast of Washington.

I found a boat operator who boasted that over 90% of his trips encountered killer whales. When I called, the kid who answered the phone said they had lots of availability on the morning I planned to grant Diane's birthday wish. I also asked him to recommend a good hotel on the island. He obliged and just to make sure it was everything I wanted, I looked up the hotel on the Internet.

Everything looked perfect. The hotel's website featured pictures of rocky coastlines, a lighthouse, boats, whales jumping and everything you might expect to find in the Pacific Northwest. I knew my wife would enjoy looking out at the ocean after a day of sightseeing, so I booked the room that, for just $25.00 a night more, offered our own private deck.

I was proud of myself for putting together all the key aspects of a perfect, maybe even romantic, weekend. For a while I completely forgot that, since I am working with the disability of being a husband, I am incapable of having anything so complicated go right.

The weatherman was saying that the weekend we planned to get away would be, at a minimum, partly sunny. Naturally, I should have remembered that the only living being that can be wrong more often than the average husband, is the weatherman.

Still, a little rain wouldn't prevent us from looking out on the marvelous vista of coast and ocean from our hotel room's private deck. A little cloudy weather would probably be more comfortable than a blazing sun when we went out on the boat.

We decided to immediately head for our hotel after getting off the ferry. I wanted Diane to start enjoying those incredible views that I had seen on the Internet. I even surprised myself that I found the road to the hotel without circling through the town several times and eventually giving in to my wife's pleas to stop, leave my manhood at the car door, and ask someone for directions.

We seemed to be driving away from the ocean, but I wasn't worried. We were going uphill. No doubt the hotel would be looking out over the ocean from a high point on the island.

Our first hint of a problem came in the form of the deer-caught-in-the-headlights look we got from the hotel clerk when we asked her to make sure our room gave us the best possible view of the ocean.

"You can't see the ocean from any of our rooms," she said in a tone that indicated we were clearly a pair of those stupid first time visitors to the island.

"But the pictures on your website gave me the impression that we'd be looking at a lighthouse on a rocky shore..." I said.

"A lot of people seem to get confused by that," she said.

When we got out on our deck, I tried to compensate for the mistake. I filled a glass of water, threw in some salt, and set it on a picture of a seal I tore from the Seattle newspaper. Somehow it didn't seem to meet Diane's expectations of an ocean view.

If we couldn't look at the ocean, at least we could get in the water in the beautiful pool and hot tub they displayed on their website. It turned out those facilities were actually in another hotel owned by the same company halfway back down the hill to the dock.

The weekend went downhill from there. We arrived at the dock ready to go out and see the killer whales, and discovered that there was no reservation in our name. The manager eventually got things straightened out and we did get to spend an hour or so with the whales. Between the boat spray and the rain, I think the whales might have been a bit drier than us.

We couldn't even get off the island without something going wrong. We decided to get to the ferry a couple of hours early to make sure we'd catch the one we wanted. When they finally started taking cars from our holding area, they said they only had room for twelve more cars. We were car twelve. Naturally car seven had a trailer. We got to be the first ones to board the ferry that left two hours later.

I'm almost afraid to think what I'll be getting for my birthday.

Section Two:
My Heart Went Pitty Pat –
And I Came To On The Floor

Neither Rain, Nor Sleet, Nor Heart Attack...

I imagine that finding someone laying on your living room floor, clutching his chest and having difficulty breathing might be somewhat disconcerting. At least I think that was what the look on my dog's face meant when she saw me doing just that.

It's curious what goes through a dog's mind when she sees her master in a situation like that. Tara came to the conclusion that I needed one of her stuffed animals to make me feel better. When that didn't have the desired results she dropped a heavy rubber toy onto that part of my anatomy that doesn't appreciate having a heavy rubber toy dropped on it, even at the best of times.

In a heartbeat I went from thinking I was about to die and wishing I would.

I'm writing this column from my hospital bed. I had a mild heart attack just before dinner last Sunday. My wife said that if I didn't feel like roast beef I could have just said so instead of trying to avoid it this way. Given the way a heart attack feels, I don't think I would recommend it for avoiding any food.

Well, maybe broccoli, but nothing else.

The adjective 'mild' in association with 'heart attack' is a bit confusing. In my mind a heart attack is a heart attack. They hurt, probably just about the same as a mild natural childbirth.

Apparently one of the arteries around my heart is blocked, despite the fact that my cholesterol level is quite low. Sometime in the next few days I will be moved to another hospital where they will insert a long tube through my groin and feed it through a blood vessel to the site of the blockage.

Thinking about the combination of the words 'insert,' 'tube,' and 'my groin' is enough to give me another heart attack.

The hospital dietician has put me on the cardiac reduced fat diet. I assumed that this would mean meals consisting of unbuttered toast and water. I'm glad to report that it isn't that bad.

Well, not quite that bad.

Of the 14 meals I have eaten since being admitted, not counting breakfasts, 8 of them have been based on servings of very dry white turkey. I like turkey as much as the next guy, but I'm beginning to feel like I have been caught in some weird time warp that sees me eating nothing but Christmas leftovers.

If I have to eat many more servings of white turkey meat I think I may start growing feathers.

To further add to my confusion, virtually every one of my 'restricted fat' meals has been smothered in gravy. I don't even eat gravy at home because it has always seemed to me to be little more than thickened liquid fat.

Most people who have had a heart attack must endure a stress test that involves walking on a treadmill with several wires connecting various points on their bodies to a medical computer program.

For the past many years I have been an incomplete paraplegic which leaves me somewhat deficient in what would seem to be a compulsory requirement for walking on a treadmill.

Like maybe the walking part.

They have a special stress test for people like me. (Wouldn't you just know it?)

It involves injecting a chemical into my bloodstream that causes my body to think it has been walking on a treadmill. The chemical also led my body to believe it should upchuck everything I have ingested since April of 1992, creating a stain on the floor of the laboratory roughly the size and shape of Vermont.

On a positive note, having a heart attack gives you access to hot and cold running morphine to deal with the chest pains.

Morphine is indeed a many splendored thing.

I don't think that it does all that much for the pain, but once it starts flowing through my intravenous tube and into my bloodstream I don't really give a flying rat's tuchus about the pain level anymore.

I will continue to file my columns each week through my recovery. Hopefully I will be able to walk out of the hospital sometime in the next week or so. Mind you if I keep eating this much turkey I might have a little trouble fitting my tail feathers in my jeans.

The Joys of Hospital Life

Living in the hospital with an intravenous tube in my arm and oxygen flowing though another tube into my nose is not without its own twisted bits of humor.

If you missed last week's column, I was rushed to the hospital after confusing my dog by dropping to the living room floor clutching my chest. She had never seen me do that in any of our games before and she didn't know what her next move should be.

I'm in a small suburban hospital. They do not have all of the equipment needed to run the tests my doctors are ordering. As a result every couple of days I am loaded into an ambulance and driven across town to be subjected to some other piece of medical technology. Most of this stuff looks like it should be run by a wild-eyed mad scientist with a humpbacked sidekick.

One of these tests was something called an echocardiogram. It's similar to the ultrasound tests that pregnant women have so that they can have a look at the fetus inside them. I've looked at those pictures before and have never had that much luck identifying any of the shapes as anything approaching humanoid. The best I've ever done was to come to the conclusion that a friend of mine was about to become the grandfather of a bouncing baby yak.

The echocardiogram also provides an accurate indication of the sound your heart is making as it (hopefully) pumps blood to your brain. People have often wondered if my heart was capable of sending an adequate supply of blood to my brain.

Others might be surprised to hear that I actually do have a heart.

I had always thought I was relatively informed about most of the body's noises. Just about everyone will tell you that the heart goes "Thump - Thump." This knowledge has largely been passed down through Saturday morning cartoons. Apparently we have been led astray all of these years. According to the echocardiogram machine, the heart sounds more like "Gursploosh - Gursplook."

It sounds remarkably similar to the sound of a toilet plunger trying to clear a major blockage in the drainpipe.

All of this riding around in ambulances can lead to experiences that I would just as soon not repeat. It was a dark and stormy morning when they drove me to the city's main healthcare facility for an angiogram. Stopped at a red light at the bottom of a hill I was able to watch, from my vantage point on a stretcher in the back, a car skid up to, but not quite crash into our rear bumper.

Thankfully for the driver of the car it didn't seem to disrupt his mobile phone call.

An angiogram, which sounds like something I might order with a nice marinara sauce, involves opening a hole in the artery in your groin, and inserting a long tube. The thought of this is enough to make my heart rate jump.

Obviously, anyone undergoing this procedure needs to have a full feeling of confidence in the doctor who will be doing the tube insertion. I had a little difficulty doing this when he came to talk to me.

Perhaps it would have been easier if he hadn't put his shirt on inside out.

The buttons were facing in, the seams were all on the outside, and the pattern said "latipsoH lareneG revuocnaV" I decided that I wouldn't point out his problem dressing himself, because, after all, he was the one armed he tube that was going into my groin.

I didn't want to distract him.

In order to do this the entire area must be exfoliated the night before. I'm not sure which is worse, the thought of the tube going in, or the razor going around that part of my anatomy. I guess I was a bit more cautious with the razor than I should have been. As a result one of the technicians said I needed a bit more shaving when they were about to start the test.

Why is it that the frumpy matronly technician isn't the one to do that?

It must be some sort of universal law that is there to test us that the cute twenty-something technician has to be the one to get up close and intimate with that area and a razor. I spent the entire time trying to think about ice-cold water, cod fish, and the frumpy matronly technician in a negligee. I didn't want her to think I was developing a hardening of my arteries in that part of my anatomy.

I'm beginning to think that if the all of the cheeseburgers I have eaten don't kill me the tests and procedures to deal with their ill effects will.

Home To My Own Bed
And No Turkey

The doctors have determined in their infinite wisdom that I am able to return home. It's been three weeks since I scared the bejeezus out of my wife, my son and my dog by clutching my chest and dropping to the floor. I'm not all that confident about going home because I am still having regular chest pains that feel like I am being pummeled with a sledge hammer.

They have loaded me down with prescriptions and told me to take it easy. Unfortunately none of the prescriptions were for the drug that made it so much easier to take it easy. I'm really going to miss the hot and cold running morphine that worked wonders on the pain in my chest, the ache in my back, and that pesky reality thing.

I must admit that I have a certain amount of trepidation about one of the prescriptions. When the chest pain and difficulty breathing strikes I am supposed to spray nitroglycerine under my tongue. While I was in the hospital the nurses applied a nitroglycerine patch on my shoulder each day. I figure that I have enough of the stuff running through my system right now to blow a sizable crater in the ground if I should fall over.

Face it, we've all learned the effects of nitroglycerine by watching that hapless coyote trying to catch the roadrunner on the cartoons. Shake it and it blows you to smithereens.

I'm sitting here right now afraid to cough.

My father used to carry nitroglycerine pills in his pocket after he had a heart attack. I was about nine or ten at the time and I can remember being very concerned that the sounds echoing through the house whenever he went to the bathroom were just the prelude to a major nitro-induced explosion.

In the early Seventies my father and I tangled with a bolt of lightening at our summer place north of Toronto. My father was knocked out by the jolt. My mother was sure he would need one of those nitroglycerine pills, so she rifled through his pockets, found the bottle, took out a pill, and swallowed it herself.

This is a woman who could go into a comatose state after taking a child's dose of Aspirin®. She had to sit down for quite a while and wasn't much help to my father or me. I don't know if dear old Dad ever got a nitroglycerine pill to jolt his heart that day, but I do remember seeing him about six feet in the air when the lightening hit. That was enough of a jolt for anyone's heart - mine included.

Obviously my actions of the past few weeks have caused a great deal of concern for my family and friends. My son took care of the job of contacting everyone to let them know what had occurred. He wasn't all together sure that first day about what the cause of my problem might have been, although he had overheard one of the doctors talking about what might be causing the chest pains. Apparently Brad couldn't remember the word that the doctor used ('angina') but he told a friend of mine it sounded like there were checking to see if I had a vagina.

I can assure you that I have not gone through a sudden radical change in my sexual orientation.

I must say it's good to be back in my own bed, even if I can't make the mattress go up and down at my head and feet like I could with the hospital bed. There's something comforting about the feel of your own bed that you can't get anywhere else. I no longer have intravenous needles poked through my skin. No one comes into the room at 6:00 AM to try to draw blood out of me. I'm not tethered to the wall by my nose with an oxygen tube, and if I have to I can get up to go to the bathroom.

Oh sure, I may not have a little buzzer to push that brings a nurse with a needle full of morphine, but on the other hand, at least when I am here at home the odds are much better that lunch and dinner won't include turkey day after day.

I guess in a way I should be thankful that things turned out as well as they did. One thing is for sure. I'm really thankful I don't have a vagina. I think that might be a little hard to explain should I ever be faced with a strip search at the border.

Is Living Without Really Living?

When a health problem sneaks up and kicks you in the butt, it gives you a lot of time to sit and think about all of the things you've taken for granted. Most of us wake up each morning and just assume that our hearts will actually be beating and our lungs will be taking in good air and breathing out morning breath.

When one or both of those expected bodily functions decides to let you know that you've been taking it for granted for too long, a lot of emotions get churned up.

Fear is a big one.

Unintentionally looking at the room from the floor definitely sets off the fear alarm. Noticing that the cardiac specialist, who is about to do an unpleasant procedure on you, hasn't learned how to put his shirt on right side out also gets the fear factor flowing. Those fears pass fairly quickly, usually around the time that the ambulance attendants take you out on a stretcher, or when they wheel you into the recovery room realizing that the doctor didn't do anything to you that he shouldn't have. Other fears aren't quite so quick to pass.

I have, for example, developed a rather intense fear about cheese.

I'm not saying that I start to shake at the sight of cheddar. I don't start to sweat if I think about Gouda. I'm not having nightmares about marauding wedges of Limburger. The cheese fear that I am feeling is based on the idea that you shouldn't eat cheese after a cardiac event.

When I think about all of the cheese that I have taken for granted over the years, I find myself missing it even more. When I asked the dietician what life would be without cheese, she said, "Longer."

Actually I think it might just seem that way.

Another rather important food item in my life has been eliminated. I have started every day of my life with grapefruit juice. Well, OK, that's an exaggeration. I don't think my mother was able to nurse me with grapefruit juice, but my reliance on it to get my day off on the right foot, started shortly thereafter. One of the drugs I am now taking came in a prescription bottle with a large warning label on it saying that I couldn't have any grapefruit while taking it.

Over the years I have had prescriptions that have been incompatible with alcohol. I could understand that restriction, and abstain, albeit a bit grudgingly, from my favorite potent potables, but the grapefruit restriction just seems a little too weird. I'm thinking that my wife may have talked the pharmacist into putting that label on the pill bottle, so that she won't keep finding the grapefruit juice container empty whenever she goes for a glass of it.

It isn't just food that I realize I have been taking for granted for the past forty odd years. Walking fifty feet without feeling like I have run a marathon was certainly something that expected to be able to do, even though I needed canes and an assistance dog to do it. These days every exertion of energy seems to leave me winded. You never really think about breathing until you find yourself only taking small gulps of air when you really feel like you need to fill your lungs to capacity.

It's been a month since I was wheeled out to the waiting ambulance, and my chest still feels like it has a rope pulled tightly around it. At times I think I am breathing by the teaspoonful.

Clearly, I've made mistakes with the way I have treated my body. If I was a car, I'd probably be parked in the back of a wrecker's lot. My air intake wouldn't be working very well, my drive train would be missing a few gears, and I'd be in desperate need of a lube. I won't subject you to any mention of what my exhaust problems might entail.

I didn't even think I was being all that hard on my body because I hadn't smoked since the Seventies. I even tried to always eat from the four basic food groups, bread, meat, vegetables, and dairy, each day. Maybe my mistake was thinking that a double chili cheeseburger with fried onions covered all four food groups at once.

Ya think...?

I Need To Book Another Time For My Allergies

It's been one of those weeks that combine a great flurry of activity with a feeling like I want to crawl under the blankets, put on a surgical mask and declare myself in voluntary quarantine. In my case SARS stands for Stupid Allergens Residing in my Sinuses.

I don't just get hay fever. Hay fever gets me.

It moves in, redecorates my respiratory system and leaves me feeling like my head has been filled with cement. I realize that there are a lot of people who think my head is already a concrete holding facility, but when the pollen starts flying, the condition is enhanced on a quantum scale. I'm not entirely certain what it is that I am allergic to, but I think it can best be summed up as June.

I'm allergic to the month.

It hasn't been too bad for the last few years. I've managed to sail through June with the occasional bout of sniffles, the odd sinus headache, and an itchy eye or two. This year is trying to make up for lost time.

Even my hay fever has hay fever.

I have all of the symptoms, and each of them has symptoms of their own. The worst of them all is having the letter 'b' take over the duties of several of the other consonants in my vocabulary. People give me strange looks when I talk. (OK, people give me stranger than usual looks when I talk.) If I go to the meat counter at the grocery store it takes a lot of sign language to finally get across that I am trying to make pizza and I need "a hab a bound ob bebberoni and a quaber-bound ob hab."

My eyes are itchy and blurry, which tends to make typing and reading difficult. Since most of my day is spent typing and reading I am only getting about half of the work done that I want to each day. I feel like I need to stop every couple of minutes and pull my eyes out of their sockets so I can scratch them properly.

Obviously I can't do that. It would make a terrible mess on my keyboard.

Being allergic to June has always been a problem. When I was young it coincided with exam time at school. On the plus side, it did offer me an excuse for why I did so poorly in French and Math. ("Gee, I guess my hay fever must have made it hard to concentrate on my studies, Mom.") Amazingly it didn't have an impact on English, history or any of the other subjects that I liked.

It spoiled more than a few camping trips, but may also explain why I used to go temporarily insane in June and decide that camping sounded like a good idea in the first place. I've sneezed and snorted through June weddings, graduation ceremonies, and my father's funeral. Just the thought of 'dust to dust' was enough set of a histamine reaction.

I've tried all manner of prescription and non-prescription medications to survive June. Once I came to the conclusion that "Take one at bedtime," really meant to take the contents of one package of antihistamines, because one tablet wasn't doing anything for me.

I don't know if that did anything for my allergy symptoms but I did sleep extremely well for the next 96 hours.

Nurses: Beware Of This Patient

Over the years I have been asked to speak to the students at a number of nursing schools. My lengthy hospital stays, after a series of car accidents in the early 1990's, has made me a bit of an expert on the patient's side of dealing with the medical profession. I refrain from telling them about the effect I have had on some of the unfortunate nurses who have come in contact with me.

If I didn't, some of the student might to choose another line of work.

One poor nurse had a great deal of trouble taking my blood pressure because the gauge beside my bed had a defective cuff. When she stretched the cuff around my arm the little hose would pop off rendering the device useless. She enlisted me to hold the hose onto its valve while she pumped.

Curiosity got the better of me on one occasion while she concentrated on the gauge with her undivided attention. I decided to carry out some medical research by finding out what would happen if I let go of the hose.

The result of my experiment was quite spectacular. She jumped about four feet straight up and eight feet backwards. The stethoscope was flung from her ears and into an acoustic ceiling tile. I guess the sound that came through her earpiece resembled what she thought blowing someone's arm off would sound like. For the rest of my stay a no-nonsense male nurse, who looked like he moonlighted as an enforcer for the mob, preformed the daily blood pressure check.

During another hospital stay I was learning how to walk with crutches after well over a year in a wheelchair. Sitting in the chair I was 4'6". Standing up I am 6'4". Height isn't my only large dimension. I am large all over my body. They used to call people like me big boned. I have big arm bones, leg bones, and I have grown a particularly well-developed belly bone since the accidents. As I have said before, the last time my dimensions fit on one of those charts that tell you what you should weigh based on your height was when my father turned to my mother and said, "What do you mean, you're pregnant?"

Often, during that particular hospitalization I would often need a painkiller in the middle of the night. One night, not wanting to disturb my roommate, I decided to "walk" down the darkened hall to the nurses' station. After several weeks in the hospital, my hair had gotten quite long and my beard was getting overgrown. Needless to say at that hour of the night I didn't stop to comb my hair before leaving my room. I put on my bright green housecoat over flaming red sweat pants and headed toward the nursing station lights. Just before I got there, the two night duty nurses stepped into the hall.

All I said was, "Oh. Hi."

You would think that a giant green and red hairy monster with four legs had stepped out of the darkness in front of them.

One danced in the same spot in a prolonged pas-de-deux. Her mouth was open but no audible sound came out. I'm sure that all the dogs within ten blocks of the hospital suddenly awoke and said to themselves, "Whoa! What the heck was that?"

The other, considerably older one proved to be far more agile than she shown herself to be in the past. In two leaps that would have made a prima ballerina proud she covered a distance of about fifteen feet into the sitting room down the hall. They spent the next twenty minutes in that combined laughing and crying mode that sudden bursts of fear can bring on.

When you laugh a chain reaction of muscle contractions occurs. First the muscle around your mouth contract causing a grin to form. Then you eyes squint and your forehead wrinkles. Just before the laughter bursts out the brain sends a message to the most important muscle in the whole process, the sphincter, telling it to contract. You can get into a lot of trouble if your sphincter fails to contract when you start to laugh.

Just ask the two dancing, leaping nurses or the one who thought she had blown off my left arm. They found out the hard way.

Perchance To Sleep

Insomnia wouldn't be nearly as bad if you could just get a good night's sleep while you have it.

Three or four times each year I go through a week or so when I just don't sleep. This has been one of those weeks.

I'm not a big fan of taking medications because I think it would be just a little too easy for me to decide that I like them more than I should. Of course it would be just my luck to take a pill with a name like Knock-U-Cold, and then have someone ask me to run some heavy machinery. Not that I have ever been asked to run heavy machinery before, but all of the directions on packages of those medications say you should avoid doing it when taking the drug, and you just know that's when someone would ask me to drive a front-end loader.

I've tried a variety of alcoholic beverages, which I already know I like more than I should, but they just leave me drunk - wide awake, and drunk. What's the point of being drunk when everyone else in the Free World is sound asleep?

Trust me. I've learned the hard way that a certain person of the female persuasion, who shall remain nameless to protect the innocent, and because I am married to her, does not want to join me at that hour. That's true when I haven't had a drink, let alone when I've poured back a few in a vain attempt to get drowsy.

It gets pretty lonely sitting up in the living room at 3:00 in the morning. Even the dog has long since fallen asleep, although she wakes up every time I move because she is trained to help me walk.

Every so often she lets out a huge groan that, despite my lack of Dr. Doolittle skills, I am pretty sure means, "For cryin' out loud, Gord... Go to sleep."

Television doesn't provide much entertainment at that hour of the morning. Jay Leno has long since signed off, leaving reruns of Matlock and I Dream of Jeanie until the paid programming takes over. I get over 100 channels piped into my home. I think 97 of them broadcast infomercials through the wee hours of the morning.

Fourteen different channels all had paid programs running that were trying to encourage me to purchase an electronic device to exercise my tummy muscles automatically. I think with the padding my tummy muscles have between them and the outside of my skin, the equipment would need to draw the same amount of power as the entire town of Lake Charles, Louisiana, before it could get them to vibrate.

One of our local channels runs nonstop scenes of bikini clad beach bunnies from two until five each morning, complete with a 1-900 number you can call to talk to someone claiming to be the goddess with the two great big, bouncing, beach balls. In case you're wondering almost 750 different clips of these girls were shown last night.

Several of the others have televangelists and fishing shows. I'm not sure which one annoys me more: the televangelist begging for money for which he will in turn ask God to cure your bunions the next time they are speaking; or, the guys on the fishing shows that land trophy sized fish and then put them back in the water.

Flicking through the channels at 3:00 AM can leave you with some images you would just as soon not see. I clicked onto one of the health channels just in time to see a surgeon remove a faulty heart valve from a patient.

I think if we were intended to see heart valves they wouldn't have been put on our insides.

I'm not sure why anyone would want to watch a home repair show in the middle of the night, but there are lots of them. I have often admitted that I am not handy with tools. In fact, given a power tool, I'd be more likely to open up an easy access to my heart valves than cut a piece of wood correctly.

My father used say that no nail in the world was in danger of being hit on the head when I had a hammer in my hands. He was exaggerating of course. I have hit many a nail squarely with a hammer. Unfortunately they were usually my thumbnails and fingernails.

I guess I'll just let this round of insomnia run its course. I won't resort to counting sheep; especially since counting the frolicking beach bunnies on channel nine is so much more enjoyable.

I'll just have to figure out whether I should be counting them by ones or twos...

Avoid West Nile Virus – Stand By Me

This whole ruckus about the West Nile Virus has me concerned. While no one in my immediate area has succumbed to the disease yet, I know that the first victim has already been selected by the advance troops of virus-bearing mosquitoes.

Me.

Anyone who is at all concerned about the possibility of contracting West Nile Virus need only stay within a couple of hundred miles of me. Proximity to me is probably safer than any vaccine that medical research could ever develop. Given the choice between biting someone close at hand (or I guess in mosquito terms that would be 'close at wing') and flying for three days to dine on my blood, most mosquitoes would chose the latter.

There are people who aren't bothered at all by mosquitoes. These are probably the same people who aren't bothered when broccoli arrives alongside their steak. In case you haven't already noticed, I am clearly not one of those people on either count.

Unlike some of the people who send me letters when they dislike something I have written, mosquitoes seem to really like me. In a group of one hundred people, ninety-nine could leave a swamp without a single mosquito bite. I would be the one bringing up the rear looking like I had chicken pox. Mosquitoes don't just like my blood. They seem to go into a frenzy whenever I am in their neighborhood.

In a way they remind me of the people who rush after the fresh crop of Beaujolais Nouveaux every year. The mosquitoes don't seem to realize that there is nothing all that special about my blood, just as the pseudo-wine connoisseurs don't realize or care that Beaujolais Nouveaux is just slightly better than Ripple.

There seems to be a co-relation between the how much one dislikes mosquitoes and how much they enjoy the soup de jour from your capillaries. Similarly, there is a co-relation between how much one dislikes broccoli and the number of times it will be served as the chef's choice.

Mosquitoes know where to find me. They charter airplanes to get to wherever I am. Those scout mosquitoes start showing up in February. It gives them time to file their reports back to the troops in time to make the rest of my year feel like one long, endless blood donor clinic without the cookies.

When the mosquitoes aren't dining on Gordon Tartar they form themselves into symphony orchestras and practice Beethoven's 5th in my ear canal. They particularly enjoy their musical interludes in darkened bedrooms where they cannot be seen, only heard.

They have also found that they can create marital discord in the middle of the night. My wife had a narrow escape the other night. She rolled over and blew in my ear. Luckily she was agile enough to duck as I sleepily tried to squash her between my palms.

I have tried most of the commercial mosquito repellants to no avail. I've also tried surrounding myself with citronella candles when sitting outside in the evening. Mosquitoes seem to appreciate it when I do that because it makes it easier for them to see me in the dark.

I am sure I will get all kinds of hate mail from animal rights groups decrying my stand on poor little mosquitoes. They will point out the important place in the food chain played by the cute little beasts. If there are birds and other beasts that need mosquitoes to fill their bellies, I will gladly donate them my share of the world's broccoli crop. If they are willing to eat something as disgusting as a bug, then broccoli should suit them just fine.

Animal rights protesters would have to take that position, lest they be seen as hypocrites. If they are going to defend all animal life they would have to include mosquitoes, not just the cute ones like seals and grizzly bears. I've often wondered how their devotion to preventing the killing or capturing of animals might change if they came face to face with a slightly perturbed grizzly bear.

Of course, I'll also have all the broccoli farmers at me again. Hopefully, they'll retaliate by refusing to sell me broccoli.

You Want To Put My What On TV?

It was definitely a good way to knock the crap out of my day – and the day before – and a good part of the next day too.

I've reached that age that makes it important to keep a closer watch on certain health issues. I've always found it quite easy to watch my weight. I just look down and there it is sitting where my perfectly rippled abdominal muscles should be.

Despite cohabitating with two teenagers throughout the Nineties, I've managed to enter the new century with my blood pressure at an acceptable level. I also watch my intake of noxious substances. I don't smoke, I drink in moderation, and I never, ever let broccoli pass my lips.

For the past twelve years though, I have been an incomplete paraplegic. I guess that's fitting, because my wife says I never finish anything I start. It means that I still have some use of my legs. It has, however meant that I have lost the feelings related to certain internal bodily functions.

On what I hoped would be a routine visit to my doctor, he decided that the time had come for a prostrate exam. I can think of no better reason to avoid visiting a doctor than the prospect of a prostrate exam. Doctors tell me that they can think of no better reason for staying home from work than the prospect of doing a prostrate exam.

The fact that neither of us enjoys it doesn't make it feel any less undignified, but I must say I'm just as glad to know that my doctor doesn't gain any particular pleasure from it.

When he had completed the task at hand (so to speak) he said that my rectal tone wasn't very good. Naturally I apologized immediately, even though I didn't hear a tone coming out of my rectum while he was rooting around in there. Apparently he wasn't talking about noises. Because of my injuries, my rectal region wasn't in top physical condition.

At least that's one way to avoid being a tight ass.

He decided that my lack of feeling in that region might make it a good idea to let a specialist have a look-see to make sure cancer cells weren't making a home for themselves in my colon.

Now it should be said that I like my doctor, and I'm not just saying that because I know he reads my books. I thought he liked me too.

Oh, how wrong I was.

Wrong, wrong, wrong, wrong, wrong.

I must have done something to really tick him off in order to give him the idea that I should be subjected to the torture of a colonoscopy. My biggest fear is that he might have sent me there with some misguided notion that I might enjoy it – not that there is anything wrong with the people who do enjoy having what feels like three miles of pressurized fire hose going in through your out-door.

The day before the scheduled unveiling of my inner workings I was told to drink a bottle of a liquid that would clear out my colon.

We aren't talking any simple, everyday, run of the mill clearing out here. I think a half-bottle of this stuff could clear out a gray whale's colon. I spent the rest of the day living in constant fear that I might be more than five steps from the bathroom when I only had time for four.

I'm going to keep this stuff in mind the next time I get a cough, the hiccups or a cold. Administering the recommended adult dose might not cure any of those conditions, but I'd definitely be afraid to cough, hiccup, or sneeze after a tablespoon or two of it.

On the morning of the procedure I had to repeat the process and drink another bottle of the human equivalent of Liquid Plumber®. I felt flushed. Not flushed in the sense of blushing, just flushed, like someone had pushed down a silver handle on my forehead.

I think it should be a rule that when someone comes in for a procedure like this, the nurse that is supposed to be helping him should refrain from pointing out that she recognizes him. Somewhere out there is a nurse who knows that she has seen a side of me I wouldn't normally reveal to my readers.

The specialist explained the procedure to me before he began. I almost wish he hadn't. The gist of it was that he would be inserting a television camera where nothing should ever be inserted. The camera was on the end of a device that looked remarkably like something I've seen a plumber use to unclog a toilet.

One possible complication is perforation in which a tear through the wall of the bowel may allow leakage of intestinal fluids, which could lead to death. Hearing that is just not a good way to keep me calm, cool, and relaxed.

He also said that it was possible that, even though I had lost some of the feeling in that region, I might have a bit of discomfort at certain points during the process.

Ya think...?

I've always marveled at how doctors can refer to something that feels like someone has set off a concussion grenade deep within your personal recesses as "a bit of discomfort..."

In actual fact, the camera itself was small enough that it didn't cause much of a problem. I think the real pain came when he tried to shove a tripod up there to steady it.

More disconcerting than the actual procedure was the fact that the whole thing was broadcast live on a color television set in front of me. I saw a side of myself that I never really ever had any desire to see. On a twenty-seven-inch color TV it was a larger than life view.

At least I hope it was larger than life...

I really expected to hear the voice of a narrator, just like those science shows on the TV channels I'm generally too squeamish to watch, "As we go forth boldly to explore where no one has ever gone before, we are witnessing the birth of a gas bubble that will eventually lead to flatulence in the patient's car on his way home. It will be of such great proportions that his dog will try to burrow through the back seat to escape into the trunk..."

In the end, well at least in that end, the test showed that I was free of the harbingers of colorectal cancer. As relieved as that makes me, it was still a real pain in the butt to get the answer.

Section Three:
Family Matters Or Is It Mutters?

Three's A Crowd

Living in a reasonably confined space with three adults can be a challenge at the best of times. At the worst of times it can bring a whole new meaning to the concept of challenging. The words needed to define that new meaning cannot be printed in a family-oriented newspaper.

When our sons were quite small we hired a British nanny to look after them while my wife and I were at work. At the time we were living in a small duplex that measured about 1050 square feet. I've always been convinced that in order to get the stated square footage as high as they did, the builders measured every conceivable square inch, including the space occupied by the mail slot.

At times the cramped quarters got to be a bit oppressive, but in general, Sarah was a joy to have around, even if she did have trouble with some of our habits and customs.

For example, no one had told her ahead of time that people in North America generally don't want to have chickens exploding in their ovens. One of the first meals Sarah cooked for us involved poultry that had to be scraped from the oven walls before it could be served. To this day I'm not sure how she did it, but at the time I had to wonder if she had her culinary training at an Irish Republican Army camp.

North American English was something that took her by surprise. While some of her ways of saying things were amusing to us, some of our ways were a downright affront to her version of the Queen's English. Having heard various members of the Royal Family speak, I still maintain that ours is a much easier version of the language to comprehend.

Some phrases were enough to turn her spine into jelly. One that always got her was the famous American university that shares its name with a cathedral in Paris. To you and I Notre Dame is pronounced "Note-Ur Dame." Sarah could never accept that pronunciation. She insisted that it was something that sounded like "Not-Rah Damn."

We discouraged that kind of language around the children.

It's been fifteen years since Sarah returned to her mother country, vowing to never say Note-Ur Dame for the rest of her life. We eventually moved into a larger house, but then, in a moment of pure insanity, decided to move into an 1100-square-foot apartment.

Just as with the builders of our duplex did many years ago, I am convinced that the designers of this palace have measured the cumulative space created by each individual shelf in the medicine cabinet to bring the total area up to that number.

Once again we find ourselves compressing the lives of three adults into a confined space. Our rather large youngest son, Brad, moved back into our home after he returned from eight months in Japan.

It's taking some getting used to. When it was just Diane and I living in the apartment, we found it small but workable. Now we find it small, cramped, and minutely undersized for our needs. We're thinking about posting a schedule showing who can be in the living room at any given time. I don't even want to discuss the splitting hairs that took place in negotiating bathroom privileges.

There is an obvious difference between sharing a cramped space with petite British twenty-one-year old female, and trying to do the same thing with a large Canadian male.

Sarah may have blown up the occasional chicken before serving it. Brad can devour the same chicken and start looking for more. Sarah could make the place look spotless before we came home from work. Brad, on the other hand makes the place look spotted.

There's a spot for his books, a spot for his clothes, and a spot for his dirty dishes.

Unfortunately they are the same spots we earmarked for the dining room table, and the china cabinet. Somewhere under the books, clothes and dirty dishes we think we might still have a dining room table, but we aren't quite sure.

I guess I shouldn't complain. After all it is nice to have him around, especially after so many months with him living sixteen time zones away. Still it is going to be awfully nice to have some breathing room again, if and when Diane and I can afford to get a place of our own.

I Hear Some People Just Eat During Mealtimes... Not Us

Two of my son's friends joined us for dinner the other night. Dining in the Kirkland household is, and always has been, an experience few forget.

We are not like the families you see on TV sharing a warm happy meal together. In our house, mealtime is riotous. It's our time to sit, go over the events of the day, and try to make others pass food or drink through their noses.

It was the same when I was a kid at home. My brother, sister, and I rarely had a meal together that didn't end in convulsions of laughter. Just about anything could set us off, and once launched my parents knew that it was probably best to fasten their seatbelts, and prepare for turbulence.

Occasionally, my mother would worry that things were possibly getting out of hand. She would warn, "Be careful, now. Someone is probably going to end up crying."

...and it would usually be Dad.

While my father seemed to enjoy the activity at the table, more often than not he tried to avoid getting caught up in the fray. If the "someone is probably going to end up crying" line didn't settle things back down to a scale similar to the Newark Riots, my mother would turn to my father and say, "Bert, speak to them."

Dad would look at each of us individually, and realizing that little he could say would have much effect on any of us, simply said, "Hi kids."

In reality, my mother was usually the puppet master who got things going in the first place. With little more than a word here or there she could orchestrate the tide and tempo of the conversation to the point where she would eventually be saying something along the lines of, "Oh my, Dear, you really shouldn't laugh with your mouth full of milk like that."

She had a scoring system. Ten points for making someone give their sinuses a milk bath, twenty-five points for passing a solid object through their nose, and fifty if the person needed to leave the table and change their clothes. There was a hundred bonus points for anything really spectacular, especially if it involved a non-family member unlucky enough to join us for the evening meal.

When my wife and I were still dating, she seemed to be a natural target for my mother's dinner-table wit. On at least two occasions, Diane put my mother into bonus point territory. There are few things more spectacular than watching a girl who is trying to make a good impression on her boyfriend's parents, try desperately to retain her composure with a banana invading her nasal cavity, through the back door.

One of those few things also occurred in the years prior to our marriage. We rarely had soft drinks around our house; so none of us knew the explosive potential of causing someone to pass ginger ale through their nose. It's the multiplying capability of all those little bubbles. To this day, my wife gets a peculiar little facial tic if anyone offers her a glass of ginger ale.

No one has ever been able to top the time my mother got my father just as he was taking a mouthful of hot coffee. We all considered wearing raincoats to the next meal.

In a few days my brother, sister, and I will be getting together for a family wedding. Our collective spouses are undoubtedly getting concerned about the thought of the three of us together at a table again.

They should be.

It's been a few years since we've all been together, and the more pressure we have to be on good behavior, the more likely an eruption of Mount St. Helens proportions will occur. My bet is that one of us will blow before we get to the "I do's."

At least the groom knows what his mother and two uncles are like, and he can steel himself for the inevitable to occur. I feel a little sorry for the bride and her family, though. Perhaps someone should warn her, but then why spoil the fun?

Are my sister, brother, and I crazy, odd, or a little bit strange? I'd have to go with a 'yes' on that one. But it isn't really a bad thing. We're probably closer than most adult siblings because we put the f-u-n into the dysfunctional world of 1960's suburbia.

You don't even want to think about the three of us sharing a pew at a funeral.

Ah, The Joys of Youth

I'm used to being the youngest. I have a much older sister and a much, much, older brother. Even my wife is significantly older than me. This is one of those years that seem to enhance the differences in our ages.

If we were all to be asked to fill out the same survey today we would be in four separate age groups. My brother would check 60 - 65. My sister would be in the 55 - 59 group. My wife, thanks to her birthday last weekend, would now be a member of the 50 - 54's. I'm in the much larger and more youthful group of people who are 0 - 49. I won't be changing age groups for a long, long time to come. If my math is accurate, my sweet days of youthfully being under fifty still have about 135 to go. That's the rest of spring, all of summer, and a bit of autumn.

Even when we were married, Diane was in a different age category. She was in her twenties when she robbed the cradle and married a mere teenager. I was in my teens for a whole 48 days after our wedding.

Being younger is both a blessing and a curse. There are just so many things that I don't have in common with all of these old folks. In the Sixties and Seventies much was made of the Generation Gap between the Baby Boom Generation and their parents. Long hair, clothing selection, music, recreational stimulants, and attitudes about peace, love and understanding seemed to create a rift between children and parents. That rift also exists between those youthful members of the under-50 crowd and our elders in the upper age brackets.

Take music for example. My wife would rather listen to John Denver than a new group like Third Eye Blind. I, being so very much younger, would rather listen to The Rolling Stones than Third Eye Blind. My much older wife likes to spend a quiet evening sitting by the fireplace. I'm far too with-it for that kind of an old-fogy activity. I'd much rather spend a quiet evening sitting by the fireplace *and* the TV.

I'm sure you can see the youthful difference in my preferences.

Diane skipped the drug culture of the Sixties, but seems to be trying to catch up in her more senior years. She's not trying to get high. She's taking a wide variety of vitamins and herbal remedies to combat aging, build up her bones, and combat those personal little heat waves that she seems to experience even if I am shivering.

I guess it's another sign of age that my wife seems so preoccupied with hair color lately. I keep trying to reassure her that gray hair is not a sign that your best days are behind you. A little snow on the rooftop doesn't mean there isn't a fire in the furnace. Still she seems to think that hair turning from dark to gray is a clear signal of membership in the old goats' association. Nothing I can say seems to change her mind. Perhaps it has something to do with the fact that she is the one who still has dark hair and mine is gray.

I think being closed-minded like that is probably another sure sign of old age. I also think that the fact that I am the one who went gray is a sure sign of which one of us is easier to live with.

I don't know about the rest of you, but I find that these older people get cranky really easily. I have been threatened with severe bodily injuries if I so much as touch the thermostat. She gets annoyed if I leave a mess in the kitchen, collect a heap of wet towels on the bathroom floor, or leave newspapers all over the living room. I'm sure that this lack of patience has to be an age thing, because I can remember my parents behaving just as irrationally after they crossed over the half-century mark.

I know I don't have a lot of time left. By the time this book comes out, I will have crossed over to the dark side of fifty. Just the other day I actually caught myself listening to John Denver. I was even more concerned when I started wondering if the ads for fiber supplements might be something I should be paying more attention.

I'll do my best to retain my youthfulness. I think I'll put a 'Born To Be Wild' sticker on my cane.

The Great Honey Bucket Disaster of 1958

I've been thinking a lot about my father lately. It's hard to believe that it's been over twenty years since he passed away. During his life he brought me a lot of laughter, not always intentionally.

He was a handyman. Somehow I didn't inherit this trait from him. I thought it might be one of those things that skip a generation, but my sons don't seem all that handy either.

His workshop contained tools that I knew only as the things that would be more likely to cut a straight line through my finger before I could make them cut a straight line through a piece of wood. Hammers, screwdrivers, wrenches, and pliers are all potentially weapons of personal destruction in my hands. Whenever I needed something done that involved any of those skills or tools, my role was usually limited to holding the nails, or passing him whatever tool he needed. I could usually be counted on to get the right tool passed to him within four or five attempts.

To this day I can't understand why he had more different types of screws in his toolbox than there were in the copy of the Karma Sutra I found in his sock drawer when I was twelve.

He was meticulous about his desire to get things just right. He didn't tolerate mistakes very well – mine or his own. Usually if the mistake was of his own making, he hoped to find another person who could share the blame, or better still, take it all.

When things didn't go just right, I could be pretty sure that I would be getting into trouble. It wasn't that I was the cause of things not going just right – well, not ALWAYS – but most of the trouble I got into resulted from my inability to stifle laughter when I'd see imperfection creep into his perfect facade.

Usually when someone goes to such great lengths to avoid being seen as anything less than perfect, their mistakes and calamities appear to be even more spectacular than those of meager mortals. Probably the best example of this, when looking back at my father's life, was the Great Honey Bucket Disaster of 1958.

Until I was about five years old our summer cottage did not have an indoor toilet. The typical outhouse was not an option either because the cottage was built on solid rock. As a result our two-holer out back had two large metal pails instead of a pit. Every couple of days my father would have to carry the pails into a forested area where he had dug a cesspool.

He had been meaning to replace the rusty handles on those old pails...

The inevitable happened on a hot July afternoon. When the first pail lost its handle, it dropped to the ground, hitting it at just the right angle to spew its contents skyward. Unfortunately, my father's left leg and arm blocked most of plume on the way up, and caught the rest on its way back down. The sudden loss of the equilibrium that carrying two fairly evenly weighted pails gave my father caused him to jerk suddenly. That motion was the last bit of strain the handle of the pail in his right hand could tolerate. It mirrored the actions of the left hand pail.

He just stood there, seemingly frozen in time. He looked skywards as if to say that, since things like that weren't his fault, a certain, omnipotent heavenly being must be to blame for his misfortune.

It wasn't often that I saw my father at a complete loss for words. Well, OK. He wasn't at a complete loss. He did manage to find one word. It wasn't "Gosh, " "Golly," or even "Darn." I suppose the word that came to his lips could have been either a curse at his misfortune or a description of what had just landed on him.

And an awful lot had landed on him.

It was one of those situations where it really didn't matter if anyone got into trouble or not. I laughed. My sister laughed. My brother laughed. When my father heard the unmistakable sound of my mother joining in the laugher, he realized he was outnumbered. He turned on his heels, walked to the edge of the lake, stripped off his clothes and threw them into the fire pit where we burned our garbage. He then calmly dove into the lake, probably killing several dozen fish with his effluent.

People weren't nearly so environmentally conscious back then.

Construction on an indoor toilet began the next morning. Reconstruction of my father's pride took a little longer.

Things That Go 'Smack' In The Dark

Halloween just isn't the same when you live in an apartment. The building association Gestapo doesn't let children trick or treat here. I miss seeing the really young ones; dressed in their costumes timidly trying to say, "Shell out! Shell out! There are witches about!" through the gaping holes where their front teeth used to be.

Of course Halloween is supposed to be a scary time. I don't ever recall being afraid of ghosts and goblins. Clowns – now that was another story. I felt somewhat justified in my childhood fears when Stephen King terrified everyone with a demented clown many years later. Those of us who knew just how scary a clown could be were vindicated by the screams in the theater during that movie.

Other times of the year can be just as scary. Try driving in my neighborhood and you'll know what I mean. My wife has had her car rear-ended three times in the past month and a half. She's almost afraid to get behind the wheel.

Looking back on my childhood, on a warm summer night, months away from October thirty-first, when I was about five years old, I witnessed pure and unadulterated terror for the first time.

We spent our summers at our family's cottage on a lake north of Toronto. Our place was only accessible by boat, which provided us with a great measure of privacy from marauding relatives who would make the hundred-mile trip north hoping to stay for a night or fourteen. On the other hand, it left us somewhat isolated from the activities in the small town on the other side of the lake.

On the night in question, my brother had decided to take in the action at the local movie theater. They were showing a number of the horror movies that were so popular in the late Fifties – The Creature From The Black Lagoon, I Was A Teenage Werewolf, Bride of Frankenstein, I Was A Teenage Bride Of The Creature From The Black Lagoon...

As my brother returned to the cottage, much later than he was supposed to be out in the boat, he needed a plan to get back without waking the rest of the family. He turned off the motor a hundred yards from our dock and slid silently the rest of the way to shore. The noise of the boat contacting the dock could just as easily have been caused by a bit of breeze or the wake of another boat.

He quietly tied the back of the boat to the rings on the dock. Perhaps it was his concentration on silence that was his downfall. His next move started a chain reaction that woke up everyone in our cottage, everyone in the neighboring cottages, and, since sound travels so well over a lake, just about everyone from one end of the two-mile long lake to the other.

Even though over forty years have passed I can still recall following my parents out the door to see what all the noise was about. Through the darkness we could make out the shape of someone standing on our dock, armed with an oar, screaming something unintelligible into the cool night air.

My brother, his mind filled with the images of creatures slipping up behind unsuspecting teenagers in the dark, was not going down quietly. No creature coming out from under the dock was going to pull him into the lake and carry him off to its ghoulish lair without a fight.

It didn't take too long to determine just what had transpired. Jim had been very successful in his attempt to slip silently up to the dock. Even tying the back of the boat had not disturbed the creature that lurked just a few feet away from the boat. It was when he stepped out onto the dock that the creature made its move.

Startled by the sudden movement, a beaver slapped its tail against the surface of the water just as Jim stepped from the boat. My brother's monster-filled mind went into hyper drive. He armed himself with an oar and started screaming. If monster movies had ever been considered a legitimate genre, Jim could have been doing an Academy Award winning screen test.

I'm not sure what ever happened to the beaver. Odds are it went deaf. As for the puddle on the dock, I'll give my brother the benefit of the doubt on that one. It's possible it could have been caused by the splash the beaver's tail made.

Possible...

I'm Lingually Confused

Some days I'm not completely sure what language I am speaking. I think I am speaking English. I hear English coming out of my mouth, but apparently others do not.

This is especially evident when I am talking to other members of my family. I could swear that I speak quite clearly and concisely, but their responses would seem to indicate that I am not. The only thing that is keeping me from questioning my own sanity on this matter is the knowledge that there are a lot of other people out there who experience the same problems.

I have had an ongoing dissertation with my oldest son for the past several months about something that he desperately needs to take care of. I've reminded him; I've reminded him that I reminded him; and, I've reminded him that I have said the same thing several dozen times. He doesn't seem to remember.

His answer is always, "Yeah, I'll do it."

In my naivety, I think, 'Yeah, I'll do it,' actually means that he will get it done. Apparently I am mistaken. If only I understood English, I would realize that it really means, "I'm saying 'Yeah, I'll do it' so that you will think I am really going to waste my time on whatever it is that you think is so freaking important."

If speaking to the generation that is significantly younger than I am seems difficult, it barely compares with speaking to the generation that is significantly older than me.

In the final few years of her life, my mother-in-law would call and ask if I know my wife's address. Since it's the same as mine, I can say with almost complete certainty that I do indeed know her address.

Giving out an address should only take a minute or two at most. Apparently I was not doing it in English, because it usually took closer to twenty minutes, by which point I am ready to rip out my own tongue.

We live on a street called McMyn Road. I believe McMyn is a Scottish name that means something to do with getting lost in the middle of nowhere. Try spelling McMyn for an eighty-something mother-in-law who has trouble hearing.

"M – C – M..."

N - C - N.."

No, M, like in Michael..."

"Oh, OK, M - C - N..."

"No, M..."

"There's no M? But you said there was an M like in Michael."

"Yes it starts with M, and it has another M too"

"MM - C- N..."

"No just one M, then C..."

"But you said there were two M's..."

That's when I would start considering the benefits of having a long rest in the home for the incurably insane - not for my mother-in-law, but for myself.

It all reminds me of an occasion several years ago, when I was working for a multinational company. I needed to call someone in one of our South American offices, but ended up attempting to leave a message with his secretary. I started to spell my name for her.

"K..." I said.

Apparently it sounded like I was saying 'what' in Spanish.

"Que...?" she said.

I thought saying 'what' in Spanish sounded like she knew I meant the letter K.

"Yes," I said, "K... I..."

"Que... Aye..." she repeated, with a strong note of confusion in her voice.

After many attempts I managed to get her through the first three letters of my name. Unfortunately that's when you get to another K, or "Que" if you prefer. It went rapidly downhill from there and I decided I could get the message to the person faster if I sent him a letter by llama, than by continuing to confuse the poor secretary with my Anglo name.

Now if only I could make my equally Anglo sons understand me, I might actually feel like I am communicating.

Yeah... I doubt it too...

You Can Have My Share

Oh the horror.

I can't imagine the level of human suffering that this is going to cause. Thankfully, the story has been played down by most of the major media. It barely got a mention on the TV news and just a couple of paragraphs in my local newspapers. The fact that I am writing about it is because of my journalistic integrity, which drives me to be sure my readers are informed of the important issues of the day.

Brace yourself.

The price of broccoli is going up.

I can assure you that I am feeling quite badly for the hoards of veggie-centric people out there who can actually eat broccoli without gagging. The fact that I am not among those people doesn't mean I am less sensitive to their plight. I've said it before and I will say it again. I truly believe that when Pandora opened that box of hers, out flew a hoard of mosquitoes, each carrying a packet of broccoli seeds under their wings.

Apparently there has been a huge crop failure wherever it is legal grow noxious substances like broccoli. When it comes to broccoli, I truly believe the word 'crop' should have a different vowel. I think an 'a' would work just fine.

My biggest concern though is that some of these people may need to find a replacement for broccoli in their diets. There might be a rush on food products that are actually edible, causing the law of supply and demand to kick in and raise the price of vegetables that I will actually willingly eat. We could be faced with rampant tomato price inflation. There might even be a rush on the supply of those beans you find in chili.

My wife is forever telling people that she can't get me to eat vegetables. She says I hate everything. That's just not true. I just hate everything that makes me gag when I put it in my mouth. OK, almost all of the things that fit into that group are found in the produce aisle of the grocery store, but there are things there that I will gladly eat. Whenever I point out that I like corn, my wife says that it doesn't count as a vegetable. She says it's a starch. She tries to say the same thing about potatoes. Corn and potatoes do not come from an animal. You don't use open pit mining to get corn rocks or potato stones. Therefore, since corn and potatoes aren't animals or mineral, they must be vegetables.

I think we can both admit that salads are vegetables. I like salads, unless you go all weird with them and add things like cabbage, artichokes, or bark mulch to them. I could be a perfectly happy vegetarian living on salads, just as long as you add lots of blue cheese and bacon, and serve them along side a nice juicy steak.

A number of years ago the People For The Ethical Treatment Of Animals took exception to one of my columns. They wrote to every paper that carried it at the time and called me a meathead. There are meat products that I choose not to eat, and I think I should get some degree of credit for that. I abstain from eating any internal organs. Despite the fact that from somewhere back in the mists of time there is Scottish blood coursing through my veins, this rule also includes haggis.

If the people that produce those reality-based TV shows ever tried to get me to eat bugs or worms, I would disqualify myself on religious grounds. I'll be damned if I'm ever going to bite into a beetle, or suck back a bowl of red wigglers. I think people who do that must spend a lot of time waiting around with baited breath.

My mother would always tell me that there were children in China who would gladly eat my broccoli. If course that's just a standard-issue maternal guilt trip, but at the time I thought that the communists must have to do a lot of brainwashing to get Chinese kids to willingly eat broccoli. I have to wonder if communist operatives, trying to weaken the will of North American children by forcing them to eat bad tasting vegetables, were somehow influencing my mother, and mothers throughout the United States and Canada.

I can see a huge benefit to the increasing price of broccoli. People think it's a lot of fun to try to feed it to me when I visit them for dinner. A joke is a joke, but not when it costs too much to pull.

I just hope they don't find out how I feel about Brussels sprouts.

Section Four:
Some Of The Animals In My Life
Have More Than Two Legs

Dogged Into Getting Some Exercise

When it comes to exercise, I maintain a very strict regimen. I've tried to adhere to it for most of my adult life. Some people might follow the fads and trends like Tai Bo, spinning, or nude cross-country jazzercise marathons. I, on the other hand stick to my tried and true routine:

Avoidance.

I'm actually quite good at it. I will do just about anything to avoid overexertion of whatever muscles still function. In my book, the last thing a guy who depends on crutches to get around needs is a sprained elbow from too many repetitions in the weight room.

I may not be firm, but I firmly believe that if humans were meant to spend their weekend running marathons, we wouldn't have invented the wheel. Don't even get me started on tri-athletes.

I can think of a lot easier ways to get sweaty than swimming two and a half miles, biking another hundred and twelve, and then running twenty-six, all before lunch.

I have always wondered why, if jogging is good for you, no one smiles when they are doing it?

My brother used to have a good system for maintaining a jogging schedule. He'd take up running in the late spring and run until the weather got too warm. He'd start up again in the late autumn but only until it got too cold. It usually meant that he would run for two, maybe three days out of the year.

My doctor keeps recommending swimming to me. Swimming can be fun if you have your own pool or live near a lake. I do not have my own pool, but I do live near a lake. The fun of swimming in that lake gets sucked right out of you before you get in past your ankles. It probably has something to do with the lake water coming right off of a nearby glacier. Swimming in a public pool has about as much attraction for me as swimming in a cesspool.

Forget the home exercise routines. The only Jane Fonda video I have ever watched was On Golden Pond. As for Suzanne Sommers, I don't mind watching her use that contraption she sells in the infomercials, but I don't think it would be safe to try watching her at the same time using the equipment. There are just a couple too many distractions when she's on the screen. I might be able to get some exercise with Richard Simmons, but only if someone held him down while I beat him with a baseball bat until he stopped shouting, "Let's sweat with the oldies!"

So I'm sure you can see the dilemma I am facing these days. A well-honed aversion to exercise is not compatible with a Labrador Retriever; especially since I am convinced that she might be part horse and part kangaroo. One does not maintain a sedentary lifestyle with a Labrador.

They don't let you.

Taking Nipper, the late, great dumbest dog to ever get lost on a single flight of stairs for a walk usually meant slowly moving down the street about fifty feet from the front door, and returning at an even slower pace. I could handle that quite nicely and not feel that I was upsetting my exercise intolerance.

Walks with my Labrador have become a combined training session, romp in the tall grass, and stop at every pillar and post to check the latest pee-mail that the other dogs in the neighborhood have left for her. These are not short little jaunts. I find that I am now spending more time outside with Tara every day than I used to in a week with Nipper. In doing so I seem to be going against my aversion to physical activity.

With Tara around, my pants have actually gotten looser. At this rate I might actually get in better shape.

All this activity does have a negative aspect. I still have to come back into my office and work after a walk, Tara on the other hand comes back into my office and promptly falls asleep. It just isn't fair.

I wonder if I could teach her to type...

The Truth About Crop Circles

Crop circles crop up in the news every so often. Those mysterious designs that appear in farm fields are a source of confusion, speculation and wonderment for some people. Those who know how they are created don't think it's such a big deal. I have recently joined this group of learned experts in the field.

There are those who think the whole thing is a hoax perpetrated by practical jokers who get their kicks by watching the public's reaction to a strange symbol suddenly covering a twenty-five acre field. That may be the case with some crop circles, but those of us who know the truth point out that they had to get the idea somewhere, and we know where they got it.

Naturally, whenever something seemingly inexplicable occurs, there will be those people who are convinced that aliens are to blame. Aliens are clearly to blame for some of the greatest scourges to hit mankind throughout the millennia. A noted astronomical journal published a paper a few years ago that indicated that life on earth appeared after our little planet drifted through a cloud of alien sewage that had been jettisoned from a spaceship in a galaxy far, far away and a long, long time ago.

Therefore, based on that bit of knowledge we can blame aliens for broccoli, parsnips, and turnips along with a great many other unpalatable vegetables. They would apparently also be to blame for mosquitoes, spiders and duck billed platypuses. Not that platypuses (platypusi?) are a scourge; I just like to fit them into a column at least once a year. Alien waste could also to be to blame for bad drivers, telemarketers who call at dinnertime, and mothers-in-law.

But not crop circles.

There are those who would have you believe that the sudden appearance of a crop circle is an omen that some god or goddess is annoyed with us. Even before I learned the truth about crop circles, I thought that idea was flawed. If a higher power wanted to let us know that he or she was ticked off with us, don't you think that they would let us know in ways we might understand? That theory might have some validity to it when applied to volcanoes, opera and movies starring Tom Green.

But not crop circles.

Some people even believe that crop circles are nothing more than the damage caused by unusual weather patterns that cause the winds to level the crop in strange and unusual patterns: mini tornadoes with an artistic twist.

While this idea does have some attraction – I'd rather see a twister draw a picture than draw a cow up to the stratosphere - it's just not the case.

The whole truth behind crop circles is much simpler than all of these theories. If I hadn't witnessed it on a number of occasions I might have not believed it myself. Crop circles are caused by something far less intriguing than aliens, gods, or winds:

Labrador Retrievers.

I bet that caught you by surprise, didn't it? Good old Labrador Retrievers are the source of those strange and wonderful designs that cover acres of farmland. Mine tries to create a crop circle two or three times a day when she is looking for a suitable spot to do her do-do.

I've had lots of dogs over the years, but none of them were ever very particular about where they left their daily marks on the landscape. Tara, the assistance dog whose job it is to keep me from falling over, is very particular. She likes the privacy offered by long grass. Luckily, we live in a semi-rural area, and there are lots of open spaces with long grass and weeds for her to make use of every day.

Long grass isn't the sole determining factor in selecting a site for her doody duty. Finding the exact location involves walking in circles over a potential spot, changing her mind, circling a new spot several dozen times, returning to the first spot for a couple of comparison laps, moving on again, until at last, after making more rotations than a high speed ceiling fan, she does what she came out to do. Upon completion, she has left an intricate crop circle in the weeds and grass.

So there you have it. Crop circles are nothing more than the paths left by Labrador Retrievers on a mission of personal hygiene. It would probably be a lot more accurate if we stopped calling them crop circles and referred to them by a name that describes what they really are:

Crap circles.

A Good Reason To Belt Your Dog

Spending a week on the road might be just the sort of thing some people might view as a holiday. For me, it's a week of appearances and a source of fodder for my columns and books.

Every time I set out on the road, I seem to run into an overload of stimuli for my unusual mind.

Driving any distance always seems to give me opportunities to speak with police officers. I may well be a traffic cop's worst nightmare - a smart ass armed with a driver's license.

I should point out that I am a firm believer in seatbelts. Although the seatbelt was the cause of most of the injuries I sustained in the car accident that left me with considerably less mobility and even less golfing ability, I probably would have been killed had I not been wearing it. Tara, my assistance dog, wears a canine seatbelt when we are traveling.

On a hot, sunny highway in the Rockies recently, we were stopped in a roadside seatbelt check. Tara is a magnet for attention from just about everyone who sees her. She wears a green vest with her service dog designation clearly marked on it so that she can accompany me into restaurants, stores, and other places that normally discriminate against canine clientele. Customs officers spend more time talking to Tara than they talk to me when we cross the border. The police officer who stopped us immediately noticed Tara before he started speaking to me.

He said, "Hey would you look at that, even your dog has a seatbelt."

Knowing that he hadn't even noticed me, or the dark sunglasses I was wearing, gave me my opportunity to play with his mind. "Yes," I said. "I want to protect her because she's my seeing-eye dog."

He nearly broke his neck quickly turning his gaze from Tara to my dark glasses, back to Tara, and back to me. I sat in the driver's seat moving my head from side to side like Ray Charles or Stevie Wonder. His chin had dropped and his eyes were wide. I knew I had an easy target.

"She barks once when I have to stop," I continued, "twice for a left turn, three times for a right, and so on."

OK, maybe that pushed it a bit too far. He realized that I was having fun at his expense. I decided I had better stop while he was still laughing and before he found a reason to give me a ticket.

Is it any wonder that a chill runs up my wife's spine whenever we stopped at anti-drunk driving checkpoint? She is convinced that one of these days, she'll be the one driving away from the checkpoint while trying to decide whether she really wants to get me out of jail for public smart-assedness.

I usually have a bottle of soda, or a drink cup from a fast food restaurant with me in the car. When the officer asks me if I drank any alcohol before getting behind the wheel, I say no, but that I had been doing a little Coke®.

I learned the hard way not to say that when crossing the border. On one occasion, I was asked if I was bringing anything back into the country, and I made the mistake of saying, "Just a little Coke®.

Apparently Customs officers don't share my sense of the whimsical. They don't share road check police officers' senses of humor either. You'd be shocked and amazed at what a ticked off Customs officer is allowed to do to the nooks and crannies in your car, and your briefcase, to say nothing of your more personal nooks and crannies.

I think I should be given a little credit for breaking the monotony that must exist for police officers checking seatbelts and drunk drivers. People like me perform an important service. After hours of hearing nothing but "Yes, sir," or "No, sir," when they stop cars, we shake things up a bit. My wife thinks it would probably serve me right if someday one of them reaches into the car and shakes things up a bit for me. After my experience with the humorless Customs officer, I have to admit that she just might be right.

But I won't let it deter me. After all, I am a professional smart ass, and Tara and I have certain standards to maintain.

That Isn't A Mutt...
It's A Great Danepoo

Life is good. Life with a dog is even better. Life with my dog is a whole lot easier.

Tara, my female Labrador Retriever, has been trained to help me with things that became more difficult after my spinal injury. She walks with me, seemingly glued to my left leg to give me some extra stability.

A lot of people still think I am pretty unstable, but that has nothing to do with my ability to stand up.

She picks up anything that I might drop so that I don't have to try to keep my balance bending over to pick it up. She can even open doorknobs and push elevator buttons when my hands are full.

Clearly, Tara works for her kibble. Other dogs in my life have made it their careers to be watch dogs (they'd watch if anyone ever broke into our home.) One thought he was a bird dog, but that just involved a neighbor's chickens. We once owned a border collie that would have liked to work herding sheep. Unfortunately, due to our complete lack of sheep, he had to make due with the cats, and on one rather spectacular occasion, a skunk.

Despite their differences all of them will go down in the annals of dogdom as equivalent in their loyalty and their ability to unconditionally love their human roommates.

That's why I find it odd that some people put conditions on their dogs. It seems that it is no longer acceptable to have a mutt, mongrel or just plain mixed breed dog. In order to be worthy of sharing the house with these people, the dog must be either a breed recognized by the American Kennel Club or some sort of invented hybrid.

It's the invented hybrids that I find confusing.

A few days ago, a woman was admiring Tara and told me that she had a Shitzapoo at home. I told her that I thought that was the place to have one because you can get all sorts of nasty germs these days if you do it in a public place. She gave me an odd look and wandered away muttering. Personally, I think I should have been the one to give her an odd look for sharing such private information with a perfect stranger.

A look through the pets section of the classified ads reveals just how many different combinations of dogs are now being given official sounding names. You have to remember that these dogs used to be listed as "cute puppies - free to a good home."

The ads now offer things like Cockeagles for $250.00 - all because a neighbor's beagle happened to drop by for a visit with the seller's cocker spaniel.

One that really took me aback was the Rottoodle. It was hard enough to picture the union of a Rottweiller and a poodle, but it also left me wondering if it was like those things you see on the Discovery Channel that end with the females eating her mates after the acts are completed.

I'll let you use your own imagination about the name someone gave to a combination of a bulldog and a spitz.

Pekihuahua puppies, which I assume must be some combination of a Pekinese and a Chihuahua, are apparently worth $400.00. I'm not sure what that combination would look like, but I expect we'll all learn if someone ever needs a spokes-dog for a combined taco and wonton restaurant.

"Si. Drop the sweet and sour chalupa."

Someone advertised a Chowador, which I took to be a kennel tryst between a Chow and a Labrador. I think that term might also be applied to virtually every dog I have ever known. My dogs have all adored their own chow and would be grateful if I'd share mine with them too.

Especially if it involved pizza.

That said, I think it's a credit to their species that I have never owned a dog that would willingly eat broccoli.

Recognize Me Recognize My Dog

Occasionally, readers will recognize me when I get the chance to escape from my office. It doesn't happen a great deal around home, because in the ten years that I have been writing my newspaper column, it has never appeared in a newspaper in this area. My readers all tend to be in cities anywhere from a thousand to four thousand miles away.

It's something that my sons were glad of during their teen years, when they were regular features of the columns. They felt a bit more secure knowing that their friends – or their girlfriends' parents – were not going to read about their exploits.

For years I have simply been known as Diane's husband or as Mr. Diane Kirkland around here. Over the past couple of years, with the release of new books and appearances on local and national television, I am starting to lose that anonymity.

My family is very, very worried.

I was on an airplane a few weeks ago, heading to a city where the column appears. The woman in the seat beside me asked if I was Gordon Kirkland. It's not something that I can easily deny, especially when so many papers have my picture at the top of the column.

When I admitted to the fact that I was indeed Gordon Kirkland, she said, "Oh. I only ever see you from the neck up in the picture in the paper. I didn't know there was so much of you underneath."

Yes, ladies and gentlemen, I readily admit that I am now, and I have always been, been big for my age. There is a great deal of me between my neck and the floor.

Sometimes I will be recognized when I am with Tara, my disability service dog. People often ask if she is the dumb dog they have read about in my columns and books.

Tara has very little in common with Nipper.

Nipper, who passed away in 2001, was a blond cocker spaniel. She quite literally could, and would on a regular basis, get lost part way up the single flight of stairs in our old home.

Tara is a cream colored Labrador retriever. She walks on my left side to give me extra stability. Anything that I drop she will pick up and hand to me, so that I don't do a pratfall into the ground trying to pick it up myself. She can also take things from the bottom shelves in stores that I point out to her and pass them to me. If my hands are full she can open a doorknob or press an elevator button. On an intellectual scale, most people who have met her think she is slightly smarter than me.

As a disability service dog, she is welcome in places that other dogs are banned from entering. Most of the restaurants that we frequent know that she is usually better behaved than me.

Still, it's nice to know that so many people remember Nipper and her ability to get lost on a single flight of stairs. I still miss her whenever I see a blond cocker spaniel.

While Nipper gave readers a sense of superiority in knowing that their dogs weren't the dumbest canine around, Tara often makes people a bit confused. Seeing-eye dogs are commonplace. Disability service dogs aren't as well known. As a result, people often think she is leading a blind man around.

I like to point out that I have a cane and a white dog, not a dog and a white cane.

A few months ago we were in a bookstore together. I heard a young girl loudly ask her mother, "Mom, what would a blind man be doing in a bookstore."

I couldn't resist the opportunity. I looked at Tara and said, "Bookstore? Dammit Tara, I said take me to the grocery store. No wonder I can't find the tomatoes."

Is it any surprise that my family was happier when I wasn't recognized?

My Name Is Not Shamu

I have always admitted to being big for my age. I don't feel particularly badly about my size. It's really just a part of who I am. I will however, admit to feeling a bit better when I see someone who makes me look thin. Traveling as much as I do seems to give me a much wider range of people to see.

And when I say "wider," I really mean wider.

I was in a very overcrowded elevator in my hotel the other day. There were two of us on board.

Three, if you count the small white dog gripped tightly against the bosom of one of the largest women I have ever seen. As I followed a rump the size of those championship pumpkins we see on the news every fall, I felt absolutely anorexic.

Yesterday though, I was reminded that I am not the smallest example of humanity either.

Picture, if you will, someone my size trying to squeeze his bulk into a skin-diving wet suit.

It's not pretty, is it? You may even wake up tonight screaming when that image passes through your subconscious dream state.

I'm usually pretty willing to try new experiences, so I booked my wife and I on a three-hour snorkeling excursion in the manatee inhabited waters around Crystal River, Florida. I was on tour in Florida that week, and I scheduled a couple of much needed days off to recover from twenty-six appearances in the previous six weeks.

When I finally got myself into the suit, I wasn't sure if I wanted to step outside of the dive shop. It wasn't out of any fear of embarrassing myself. At 6:45 in the morning there weren't too many people around to see me dressed in a skin tight (with emphasis on the word 'tight') black and gray rubber suit.

Dressed like that I was concerned that someone from Greenpeace might see me and try to tow me back out to sea to rejoin my pod.

We had been warned that May was not the time of year that we would see a lot of manatees swimming in the river. I was not overly concerned though because I was just looking forward to snorkeling again after a great many years.

We pulled away from the dock and within five minutes our guide was bringing the boat to a stop amid a group of manatees.

I had seen pictures of manatees, but was not quite prepared for the sheer size of the beasts. The baby in the group probably outweighed the woman I saw in the hotel elevator.

But just by a little bit.

We swam with a pair of the animals for over an hour. We were joined by a group of German tourists from another boat. As I swam along beside a manatee, I felt something pull me backwards and away from it. My immediate thought was that one of the state's other large animals, an alligator, was taking me home for lunch.

As I don't have much feeling in my legs due to the spinal injury, I could not tell whether it was teeth cutting into me. All I knew was that something had tugged me backwards with a great deal of force.

It turned out to be something much more ferocious than an alligator. It was a woman from the group of German tourists. Luckily I was able to free myself from her grip and swam away, granting her wish for an unimpeded view of the manatee.

A third manatee joined us, and I followed it, thinking the rest of the group was doing the same thing. After a few minutes I discovered that I was alone with two very large female manatees. The rest of the humans were a hundred yards away, still swimming with the original pair.

The manatees were as curious about me as I was about them. They may not have been used to a human of my size. In my wetsuit, I might have looked like a manatee, too.

I made a hasty retreat back to the other swimmers when the bigger one made it clear that she really liked me.

She really, really liked me.

Fluffy, Leaves A Large Family To Mourn

To every thing there may be a time to live and a time to die. We all must go to that great unknown sometime, leaving friends and family behind. Often we only learn of someone's passing through the obituary pages in the daily newspaper. It's important to let the world know that a loved one has gone.

I guess it's just a natural extension that a number of newspapers have started providing space for the bereaved to announce the passing of their pets.

Don't get me wrong. I love my pets; those that are with me now, and those that have come and gone over the years. I wouldn't want to have gone through this life without them. I'm just not sure that a published obituary is the best way to remember someone like the late, great dumbest dog to ever get lost on a single flight of stairs.

There's just too much potential for people to get a little over the top with what gets put in the obits. For example:

Smith, Tom ("Fur Ball")

Tom came to the end of the last of his nine lives surrounded by his human family. He leaves behind an indeterminate number of kittens from his frequent relationships. He will be remembered for his late night vocalizations on his family's backyard fence that always garnered him a large audience of sleepy neighbors.

Abercrombie, Rex

Rex Abercrombie left us suddenly on Thursday when he mistook the puddle of antifreeze in a neighbor's driveway for drinking water. In his own way he managed to live more in his few years on Earth than many dogs can in a full lifetime. He was renowned throughout our neighborhood for his ability to mark his territory on anything that wasn't moving.

McDonald, Hamish ("Little Hammie")

Little Hammie passed suddenly from this life in a tragic cage wheel accident last Tuesday. He had been enjoying his daily exercise routine when he somehow managed to spin himself to death. He is predeceased by his brother Big Hammie, who died just last week after getting stuck in one of the tubes connecting his cage with the other parts of the hamster system, and by his special friend Tidbit, who last month had a close encounter of the feline kind.

Peplowski, Polly

Polly can now soar with the eagles as she enters the next life, free of her earthly wing clips. Her lifelong love for crackers finally caught up with her when she sadly choked to death on a soda biscuit last week. Her loving owner found her on the bottom of her cage. There will be a memorial service for Polly at her residence tomorrow, at which time she will be interred in a shoebox in the back yard.

Roberts, George ("Mr. Bubbles")

George passed away in his sleep and was found floating at the top of his fishbowl this morning. After a brief service attended by his family, he was flushed into the next life.

Horner, Princess

We are saddened to note the passing of our Princess on April 18, 2002. Her suffering has now ended. In lieu of flowers, a donation in Princess' name to the Center for Catnip Addiction Treatment would be greatly appreciated by those closest to her. Princess struggled with her substance abuse problem, but succumbed under the influence when she discovered that cats really can't fly even if they launch themselves from a thirty-seventh floor balcony. Despite her problems she always landed on her feet, even at the very end.

Douglas, Spot ("Spotmeister")

The Spotmeister died just the way he would have wanted to - in the midst of one of his favorite activities. Even though the neighbors didn't care for having their cars chased by Spot every time they passed our house, he took such great pleasure in the game that we just couldn't bring ourselves to make him stop. Unfortunately, Spot succumbed to the injuries he sustained when he collided with a 1957 Volkswagen that ventured onto our street. He had never actually caught a car before.

Binghamton, Baron Jacques de Rothchild III

Our beloved Baron Jacques has disappeared, leaving us to assume the worst. He had never left his silk pillow before, but for some reason slipped out a window that our former maid left open. (She never liked dear Jacques.) Being totally unprepared for life without his daily caviar and truffles, we fear that he must surely have become disoriented and starved to death. Thanks go to his canine psychologist Dr. Frankie for his help getting us through our time of loss and sorrow. Donations to the Center for Poodle Genetic enhancement would be an appropriate way to remember Baron Jacques.

Cartwright, Ben

Ben the python slithered into the next life last week, after choking on my uppity neighbor's stupid poodle.

Back In The Saddle Again

It's now been just over fourteen years since I broke my spine. In that time there have been a lot of things that I have had to put into my well-I'm-not-going-to-do-that-again file. Surprisingly, as time passes, I have managed to pull a few things back out of that file.

A few years ago I wrote a column about one of the things that I miss most from my life before the accident. Some readers only read the first paragraph of that column and for some reason thought I was talking about something entirely different.

I can't imagine why.

It said, "I miss the feel of hot, sweaty flesh, pounding rhythmically beneath me, and the sounds of heavy breathing and snorting as I arc up and down - at times barely able to avoid falling off. I miss the rush it gave me as it forced adrenaline through my system. It's not that I experienced it very often, and, frankly, I wasn't all that good at it, but every time I did it, I had a great time. Had I known that I'd have to stop doing it, I would have done it a lot more when I could. That's why I find it hard to believe that there are people out there who have no desire to even try it. I'm sure some of you just take doing it for granted. I did. I now wish I hadn't, of course."

Naturally, I was writing about horseback riding.

I recently mounted up again for the first time since the accident. I was invited to go for a ride at a local disabled riding center.

It's been often said that the best thing for the inside of a man is the outside of a horse. I'd like to verify that statement. Getting back onto a horse was one of the best experiences that I have had in a long, long time, even if I did approach it with a certain degree of apprehension. Just standing with the large horse before my ride brought back a lot of memories. There are few experiences that can compare with having a horse press her head against yours, letting you know that she is pretty sure you have an apple or two in your pockets.

OK, so my ride wasn't galloping along a dusty trail with the wind in my face. She was just walking around in an indoor riding ring with two aides acting like training wheels on either side of me, but I was riding.

Best of all, I didn't fall off.

Those who have seen me know that I am not a small man. I've never ridden small horses. Putting me on a Shetland pony would look like a western version of the Shriners on their little motorcycles. The horse I used to ride was half Belgian and half Standard bred. Few other people could get their legs around his ample girth. The horse I was given to ride last week had similar characteristics. She was mostly Percheron, a breed better known for pulling wagons than supporting riders.

We fit together perfectly, although it did take me a few minutes to get back the proper rhythm needed to keep certain sensitive parts of my anatomy from sustaining a bruising or worse.

The only downside to the whole event was the helmet I had to wear to keep the insurance companies happy. It looked like a black velvet construction hardhat. I felt - and probably looked - like the construction worker from The Village People.

Even the horse seemed to be laughing when I put it on.

I Like Horses, But It's Platonic

I spent the weekend doing an appearance at a resort nestled beside a lake in the mountains. While I worked there getting my audiences to laugh at the stories I use in my act, I was also apparently getting laughs back at home.

I told you in the last chapter about getting back into the saddle again at the local disabled riding stable after so many years of missing the feelings of freedom on the back of a horse.

They asked me if I would mind having the press come out to watch one of my rides. Despite feeling somewhat ridiculous wearing the black velvet hiding helmet, I agreed.

I see now that it might have been a bit of a mistake.

One of our local newspapers sent a young girl to do the story. I've been misquoted in the press before, but never quite so spectacularly. I had even called her the next day to see if she had any points she wanted to clarify for her story.

When the paper hit the stands back home, my son called me at my hotel.

"Uhh... Dad," he said, "you might want to have a chat with the newspaper when you get back. There's a story in it about you and it makes you sound a bit perverted."

Perverted?

I've been made to look crazy, even insane, in the past. I've had articles written about me that made people wonder how my wife has put up with me for so many years. There have even been a couple of stories that made it painfully clear to the readers that I am not of average build.

But perverted...? That's a first.

When discussing riding, I often use a quote from Lord Palmerstone. He said, "The best thing for the inside of a man is the outside of a horse."

It's true. Riding on a horse is an exceptionally wonderful experience. I had missed it a lot, and thoroughly enjoyed my chance to get back on one. Unfortunately the intrepid reporter didn't write the quote down properly, didn't bother to double check its accuracy, and didn't stop a lot of people around home from wondering just what I was really doing with - or to - that horse.

She wrote, "The inside of a horse is healthy for the outside of a man."

As my son said, "Dad, it makes it sound like you were doing something that would probably get you kicked."

He's right. It's a big mistake and it does make me sound somewhat perverted. I want to make it perfectly clear that, while I like horses, it's strictly on a platonic basis.

Rearranging what I said in that way would be like referring to a Rolling Stones' song as "Hey, Hey. McLeod, McLeod. Get Off Of My Ewe."

Garrisson Keillor once pointed out that writers don't really have bad experiences it's all just new material. This proves it. Being made to look like I have a different sort of passion for horses has given me this column, and some new material to use on stage. I might even be able to write a few book sequels. I could change just one word in the titles of books like *The Horse Whisperer* and *They Shoot Horses Don't They?* I'll leave you to decide what words to insert into *The Horse Blank* and *They Blank Horses Don't They?*

I've had several calls so far from so-called friends, who want to take advantage of my new public image as someone who has a peculiar and unnatural interest in horseflesh.

You'd think people could just let something like that slip by.

But, no...!

When I asked one of them why he got so much joy out of seeing me described that way in the press he asked if I would ignore it if the article had been written about him.

Well, of course not.

If I saw one of my friends misquoted to the point of being made to look perverted, it would just be wrong for me to ignore it. But that just goes to prove my point about humor in general. If something unpleasant, embarrassing, or even mildly painful happens to someone else, then it is funny.

If it happens to me, it's not funny.

And I just wish people would start to understand the difference.

Attack Of The Mutant Cricket

I've often written about my wife's fear of spiders. It doesn't matter whether it is a giant bird-eating tarantula or an eight-legged creepy-crawly thing that you practically need a microscope to see; they all scare the bejeepers out of her.

It doesn't even have to be a real spider. A toy plastic one, or even a picture of one in a magazine, can send her over the edge. National Geographic magazine is no longer welcome in our house after that nasty spider-on-the-cover incident a few years ago.

I can't say that I am a big fan of spiders or other bugs that go bump in the night. If they are just normal every day flies and bugs, I can tolerate them for as long as it takes me to swat them into oblivion.

It's the mutant ones that get to me.

I arrived in Atlanta a couple of weeks ago in the midst of a horrendous downpour. It rained so heavily that the interstate buckled from the excess water. It was a long slow drive. The last fifty miles took me nearly three-and-a-half hours. All I wanted was to get to the safe confines of my hotel room.

Apparently several crickets also had the same idea.

I've had crickets in a hotel room before. They are not welcome roommates in my book, because they do cricket karaoke serenades in the middle of the night. They are almost as annoying as the lizard that climbed the wall of my hotel room in Thailand. In the middle of the night, when it called out for a little female lizard companionship, it made a noise that you'd expect to hear in a Stephen King movie.

I found two crickets doing freestyle swimming events in my toilet bowl. They weren't the normal, everyday crickets that I am used to seeing. Crickets are supposed to be small, certainly not more than a half an inch long.

These things were huge. They were the cricket equivalents of Kobe Bryant - definitely not welcome guests in my hotel room.

They were dispatched with a flick of the flush handle, although one of them was nearly able to swim against the current.

I was tired from the drive and headed to bed without further thought of crickets.

In the middle of the night I was awakened by a strange sensation on my leg. I don't have much feeling in my legs and, whatever this was; it was north of my knees and heading further north.

That's when I remembered the King Kong Crickets.

I'm not ashamed, and comfortable enough in my manhood, to let you all in on a little personal secret.

In situations like that I am perfectly capable of screaming like a little girl.

Remember, we aren't talking about a cute Walt Disney character here. It didn't have a top hat, and it wasn't about to stop and sing When You Wish Upon A Star.

With the speed and direction it was heading, I am pretty sure it was planning to have its way with me.

It might have just been my imagination, but I am pretty sure I heard it growl when I knocked it off my leg. I grabbed one of my crutches and, thankful for those fencing lessons I took as a kid, parried and thrust the beast into the rug.

I remembered from my high school biology classes that crickets can sometimes play dead and then scamper away. Despite the large pool of cricket guts that spread across the rug, I continued to beat the thing for a good five minutes.

When I told a Georgian friend of mine about the incident the next day, she gave me a look of horror. At first I thought she was being sympathetic to the fright I had received in the night, but of course you all know my track record with accurately reading the look on a woman's face.

"You didn't kill it did you?" she asked.

"Spreading a cricket into a carpet stains the size and shape of Rhode Island is generally fatal'" I said.

"But you're not supposed to kill them," she cried. "It's good luck to have a cricket in your room."

Not for the cricket.

When Good Bears Go Bad

One of my concerns working in this business is that readers often do not hear the important stories that get overshadowed by the media's intent on covering the trivial items like war, famine, pestilence, and the inability of certain world leaders to pronounce words the rest of us learned in kindergarten.

As a result, from time to time, I like to dedicate a column to these important world events that you might have missed.

When those stories involve beer, it's just an added bonus.

Recently, a black bear in Washington State that was incarcerated on a charge of P.U.I. (prowling under the influence.)

We've all heard jokes starting with the line, "A bear walked into a bar..." In this case the bear walked into a campground and started pulling cases of beer from campers' coolers in the middle of the night.

The region had been experiencing a couple of weeks of unusually hot weather. I guess even bears know that there is nothing quite like a beer pulled out of icy water on a hot day.

According to the report that came across my desk last week, Lisa Broxson, a worker at the Baker Lake Resort, 80 miles northeast of Seattle, said, "We noticed a bear sleeping on the common lawn and wondered what was going on until we discovered that there were a lot of beer cans lying around,"

In fact, the bear was surrounded by three dozen empty cans of Rainier Beer. There was also one partially consumed can of Busch, tossed aside after a couple of swallows. The bear clearly preferred the taste of Rainier.

The bear was chased away by wildlife officials. It climbed a tree and went back to sleep. It returned to the resort the next day. Video tape I saw of the bear clearly showed that it was still under the influence. Wildlife officials decided to trap the bear. They opened the trap door and threw in some donuts.

The bear didn't move.

They added marshmallows.

The bear didn't move.

They turned to the only sure thing that would get this bear into the cage. When they put in some Rainier beer, the bear staggered in and sat down. It was taken far into the wilderness and released to sleep it off.

In further researching the story for your enquiring minds, I found a quote from Jen Scott, Rainier's public-relations agent in Portland that made me wonder if the story had been an elaborate stunt.

She said, "I swear to God, we had nothing to do with it."

Of course you all know that when a public relations agent says something like that it really means, "We held a casting call for alcoholic bears a few weeks ago. Bruno here really impressed us with his ability to consume our client's products. He also did a really great job following the script, especially the part about throwing away a half a can of Busch. I see a great future for him in commercial work. John Kerry's people have been in touch to have Bruno join the Democratic campaign because no matter how you spell it he doesn't like Busch."

The people at the Baker Lake Resort should be glad it was just a bear. After I heard this story, I wondered if there had been other cases of animals developing a taste for beer.

Apparently, elephants become nasty after a few beers.

In 1999, a herd of 15 elephants descended on a village in the Assam region of northeastern India, broke into a cluster of thatched huts, guzzled several casks of beer and then tore the village apart.

In that story, wildlife official and elephant expert Kushal Konwar Sharma reportedly said, "After drinking the beer, the elephant herd became intoxicated and went on a rampage, trampling to death four members of a family,"

It just goes to show you that you should never shout, "Last call for alcohol" when you have a hut full of drunken elephants.

At least bears know when it's time to take a nap.

I just wouldn't want to be anywhere nearby when a hung-over bear wakes up and finds out he's a hundred miles from home with no money for cab fare.

Section Five:
I Love Humanity – It's People That I Have Trouble With

You're A What...?

I need to get something off my chest about the way my profession is perceived out there. Being a fulltime writer is an odd profession. I don't find it all that odd, but it seems just about everyone else does.

Mind you, that can describe a lot of things in my life.

"What do you do?" is one of those questions that always come up when people first meet, when applying for a car loan, or when having a conversation with a police officer or border guard.

"Writer," is never the answer they are expecting, or for that matter willing to entirely believe. There are so many answers that they would prefer to accept like salesperson, septic tank redecorator, or international man of intrigue.

Writer is just not supposed to be someone's profession. Some people get an odd look that is easily translatable. Others come right out and say it.

"Yes, but what is your real job?"

I understand where the perception comes from. In cities like Los Angeles writing is something that you do when you aren't driving a cab or waiting on tables. On the other side of that coin, just about everyone in Los Angeles who drives a cab or waits on tables is writing a screenplay or twelve.

Many years ago, Margaret Laurence, a prolific Canadian writer spoke to one of my university classes on this very topic. She related the story of being at a dinner party and having the complete stranger seated beside her ask the "What do you do?" question.

When Ms. Laurence told him she was a writer, he said, "Oh. I've often thought I might give that a try when I retire."

Used to this sort of a reaction, she asked him what he did. He told her that he was a neurologist.

"Isn't that a coincidence," she said. "I've often thought I might give that a try when I retire."

The neurologist typifies the reaction most of us in this profession have become used to. Many people view writing as a hobby – something people do if they aren't smart enough for stamp collecting.

I was once asked, "Are you trying to find a real job?"

"No," I replied, "Are you and Dorothy going down the yellow brick road to try to find you a real brain?"

One that really threw me was, "It must be nice that your wife has a successful career so you don't have to work."

It's been three or four years, but I am still trying to understand how the person who said, "Oh. I didn't realize that you're gay," came to the conclusion that all writers are gay. I was just as glad he did, because it kept him at the opposite end of the room from me for the rest of the night.

My wife says I was just being cruel when I kept winking at him whenever we made eye contact.

I was at a gathering this past weekend, and happened to overhear a conversation between two people who didn't realize I was within earshot. One said that she heard that I was "some kind of a writer."

"Well," said the other woman, "he can't be very good, because I've never read anything by him."

I'd like to think that means the only people who are good writers are the ones who write the captions at the bottom of the pages of her coloring books.

I was asked to complete a survey of writers a few months ago. When I came to the inevitable question about income, I found that the top income category in the possible answers was $5,000.00." I thought I must have been missing the page with the rest of the income categories.

I wasn't.

Apparently, writers are all supposed to be poor, ravaged souls, churning out their words in lonely writers' rooms. Someday I hope I am as poor as John Grisham or Stephen King, or if I get really successful maybe even the woman at the party on the weekend will have heard of me.

My wife just hopes I don't have to become gay first.

Laugh And The World Laughs With You... Shrug And They Go Nuts

From time to time we all suffer from a bit of road rage. Most of us have the mental stability not to act on it, but there are those who feel it is their sworn duty to go off the deep end every time they get annoyed on the road. Unfortunately that is the only deep end those people ever experienced.

It's clear they came from the shallow end of the gene pool.

I met one last weekend whose lineage probably didn't even trace back to the puddle on the sidewalk near the shallow end of the gene pool.

My own personal venting of distain for the acts of other drivers on the road usually is limited to the use of the horn and the odd physical gesture. I've often thought it would be nice to have a public address system mounted under the hood of my car so that I could tell people exactly which brand of candy coated popcorn I think they may have found their driver's licenses.

I guess I displayed my disdain for the wrong driver the other day. Perhaps the fact that he was driving the cab of a semi-truck, while I was behind the wheel of my wife's sporty little compact might have given him the idea that he was more important than me. It obviously gave him the impression that yield signs were not meant for people like him. He must have thought that it meant that everyone else on the road had better yield to him, even if it meant slamming on their brakes while he cut across in front of them.

That's why I made my little gesture.

It wasn't the classic nonverbal gesture that you might be thinking of. I simply gave him one of those shrugs that silently, but effectively, conveys the message about him getting his license from the aforementioned candy-coated popcorn box.

That's when he made his own gesture of choice.

He didn't use his body parts to indicate his feelings. He used his truck. He started by slowing down in an effort to make me pass him. Since I was planning on making a right hand turn a couple hundred yards ahead, I didn't take his bait. When he eased his truck onto the shoulder of the road, I had no choice but to pass.

That's when he made his verbal pronouncements that left no doubt in anyone's mind how he felt about me.

If only he had left it there, it would have saved us all a lot of time. But no-o-o-o-o-o-o! That's when he decided to chase me.

He chased me around the corner; tailgated me as I turned into a plaza; and continued chasing me as I took a leisurely drive through the gas station lot, around the fast food restaurant, back through the parking lot, and into the drive-through lane of a donut shop. His truck wasn't going to fit into the drive-through lane, so he left.

...or so I thought.

He was just waiting for me on the other side of the restaurant. When I got to the pick-up window, he drove his truck into the lane, blocking me in. He jumped from his truck and started screaming at me that I had no right to shrug at his driving prowess. He told the server to shut up when she told him to move his truck and continued to scream at me.

Remember what kind of restaurant I said this was? Who is going to be inside a donut shop at any given time of the day or night? That's right boys and girls, and it only took a moment for the five police officers inside to come to my rescue. I don't think they were too happy to leave their crullers and coffees behind to deal with a trucker who goes nuts if someone points out his driving shortcomings with a simple little shrug.

The police later told me that that he was upset because of some family problems. Perhaps he's part of the Charlie Manson Family. Maybe he owes someone in the Soprano Family money. Then again it could be that his mommy used to shrug at him when he did something stupid.

There is a lesson to be learned in all of this. Never tell a trucker what you think of his driving unless there's a donut shop or a police station nearby.

The Earth Is Moving
And I'd Like To

We've had three earthquakes in our area in the last week. According to the Richter scale they have measured 4.5, 5.9 and 6.4. Thankfully they have all been off the coast so there haven't been casualties or structural damage.

Naturally, this tends to make me worry a bit. Between the earthquakes and the chain of volcanoes that includes Mount St. Helens that runs past here, I am convinced that at some point in the not too distant future, I will be living in my own, real-life disaster movie.

Forecasts for the West Coast are always calling for sunny periods with scattered tremors and occasional ash and lava downpours with scattered buildings and bridges.

In 2001, Mount Baker, the closest volcano to my home was venting a great deal of steam. Someone-very-intelligent-who-knows-what-he-is-talking-about said it wasn't anything to worry about because there hadn't been any earth tremors to go along with it.

With that, we were hit by an earthquake that registered 6.1 on the Richter scale, and caused a great deal of damage in Seattle and the surrounding area.

The worst earthquake I have experienced was actually just an aftershock of a much larger quake that had hit the Mojave Desert a few days before I was driving through the area. It wasn't the intensity of the quake that made it so memorable. It was my location at the time it hit.

Sitting on a toilet in a highway rest stop is not the best place to be when the earth starts to move. The partition walls shook. The toilet made a peculiar gurgling sound, and I was convinced I was going to die like Elvis – sitting on a toilet with my pants around my ankles.

I apologize if it takes you a while to get that image out of your head.

Someone-very-intelligent-who-knows-what-he-is-talking-about always comes on the news after these events and says something along the lines of, "The tectonic plates consist of an outer layer of the Earth, the lithosphere, which is cool enough to behave as a more or less rigid shell. Occasionally the hot asthenosphere of the Earth finds a weak place in the lithosphere to rise buoyantly as a plume, or hotspot."

Well, that certainly makes it all perfectly clear, doesn't it?

Someone-very-intelligent-who-knows-what-he-is-talking-about has been very quiet about this recent blizzard of earthquakes. As a result, the media has been having trouble getting one of those sound bites that the-rest-of-us-who-aren't-nearly-so-intelligent can't understand. They've had to turn to the average person on the street for an explanation. These have ranged from a woman who is convinced that God is warning us all to stop sinning to a man who thinks that the earthquakes are all part of a secret government experiment.

I, of course, have my own explanation.

It's my new upstairs neighbors.

I think it's a man, a woman, and a herd of cattle.

When they walk, their feet hit the floor with an intensity that can shake the pictures on our walls. I'm not sure if they are walking, or moving around their unit on pogo sticks.

It makes us feel like we are living inside a bass drum.

Pa-rumpa-pum-pum.

I picture them walking around their apartment using steps like the ones that the red-coated, bearskin hat wearing soldiers use during the changing of the guard outside Buckingham Palace. Occasionally they change to the steps that the Kremlin guard used just to throw a little variety into their percussion.

I am convinced that they are the cause of the recent upturn in earthquake activity in the region.

I've tried asking them ease up on the intensity of their footsteps, but that had little or no impact. Their impact with the floor remains just as intense as it was before I spoke to them.

I guess I shouldn't have gotten my hopes up about getting the message across to them that their footsteps are making my life a living hell. The couple seems to be at the opposite end of the intellectual spectrum from someone-very-intelligent-who-knows-what-he-is-talking-about. The husband makes Homer Simpson look like a candidate for Mensa.

They tried to tell us that it is the two-year-old that is pounding on the floor. Somehow I doubt that. Any two-year-old that can rattle the pictures on the walls downstairs would have to be destined for a career as a sumo wrestler.

The occasional earthquake is not enough to make me consider moving away from the West Coast. Listening to the upstairs neighbors' footfalls is making me reconsider apartment life.

Again.

Pa-rumpa-pum-pum.

And again.

Michael Moore, The F-Word, And Me

I'm glad I don't wear baseball caps.

I'm 6'4". I carry a fair amount of excess bulk on my frame. I have a full beard with more gray than black in it.

Face it. If I add a baseball cap to all that, I look more than a little bit like Michael Moore; so much so, that I have been asked by complete strangers if that is who I am.

For some reason the crutches I walk with didn't give them a clue. Perhaps they thought that the militant wing of the Republican National Committee had caught Michael Moore in a dark alley.

Before you get concerned that I am breaking my own rule about not writing about politics, don't worry. I'm not going to publicly take sides in the Fahrenheit 911 argument. I was never that big a fan of Ray Bradbury's books, so why would I comment on the movie version of one of them, even if they have upped the temperature from Fahrenheit 451 to Fahrenheit 911..

As someone of similar proportions though, I feel I have speak up on Michael Moore's defense when it comes to the way he is being talked about. For some reason, the people who don't like him have lowered themselves to using the f-word when they talk about him.

Highly placed members of the Republican Party have used it.

Church leaders have used it.

My more conservative column writing colleagues have used it.

If they can use the f-word, I guess I can use it in my column, too.

Fat.

According to an article I read last week, Michael Moore has been getting that particular f-word thrown his way quite a bit lately.

He attended the Republican National Convention as a columnist for USA Today. He was greeted by delegates calling him a "fat pig." I guess that was easier to chant that quoting Senator John McCain calling him "a disingenuous filmmaker."

That just doesn't roll of the tongue as easily as the f-word.

Calling him a fat pig doesn't require a dictionary search either.

The article I read quoted an on-line columnist, Andrea Harris, who referred to Moore as, "Fattyfatfat, Fatty McFatperson, Three Big Macs Corpulent Sack of Fat"

I wonder what she really thinks.

It reminds me of the kids in the schoolyard who used to deride anyone who was carrying a bit of extra weight as "fatty, fatty two by four..." I've always thought that people like that should all just go fat themselves. Who the fat do they fatting well think they are?

I've often admitted to being big for my age. I've always been bigger than average. I was one of the kids who had to buy jeans in the 'husky-boy' section. I now shop for clothes in places with the word "big" in their names. They know that they wouldn't have great marketing success if they called themselves something like Clothes For The Fattyfatfat, Fatty McFatperson, Three Big Macs Corpulent Sack of Fat Guy.

Inside those stores the clothes sizes are in multiples of extra large. I am not large. I'm not extra large, or even one or two times extra large. I buy my shirts in the 3XL or 4XL sections. My guess is that Michael Moore does the same. We aren't the smallest guys who go into the stores, but we aren't the biggest either.

An 8XL leather jacket could put an entire species onto the endangered animal list.

A few years ago, scientists discovered that human fat was full of stem cells that could be used as the building blocks for so many medical developments, like creating replacement organs. Some of us just have more potential kidneys and livers than the rest of you. We certainly have more heart than those who decide the only way they can deride someone is to refer to their supply of potential stem cells.

So for all of us who are overweight, plump, chubby, stout, portly, heavy, big, corpulent, obese, and dare I say, fat, I'd like to pass a message on to all of the people who think that size is the only, or the easiest, way to insult Michael Moore for his filmmaking, whether or not you think it's disingenuous.

Fat off.

Just Call Me The Rev.

I wonder if God is trying to tell me something. I realize theologians say that God works in mysterious ways, but I never thought He would resort to stuffing my email program's inbox with invitations to become a minister.

So far this week I've received twelve emails with subjects like, "Become A Minister," "Perform Weddings," and "Do God's Work."

The messages are all filled with select words and phrases in capital letters. I guess that is to be expected, because we all know that God speaks in capital letters. It tends to give His pronouncements more authoritative appeal. Who would pay attention if he transcribed His commandments on a rock in tiny lower case letters, or if He dotted his 'i's' with smiley faces or tiny hearts?

No matter what the subject line states, the messages are identical, and start with the somewhat intriguing line, "Minister Charles Simpson has the power to make you a LEGALLY ORDAINED MINISTER within 48 hours!!!!"

The rest of the note goes on to say, "BE ORDAINED NOW! As a minister, you will be authorized to perform the rites and ceremonies of the church!!

WEDDINGS - MARRY your BROTHER, SISTER, or your BEST FRIEND!! Don't settle for being the BEST MAN OR BRIDES' MAID. Most states require that you register your certificate (THAT WE SEND YOU) with the state prior to conducting the ceremony.

FUNERALS - A very hard time for you and your family. Don't settle for a minister you don't know!!

BAPTISMS - You can say "WELCOME TO THE WORLD!!!! I AM YOUR MINISTER AND YOUR UNCLE!!" What a special way to welcome a child of God.

FORGIVENESS OF SINS - The Catholic Church has practiced the forgiveness of sins for centuries **Forgiveness of Sins is granted to all who ask in sincerity and willingness to change for the better!!

VISIT CORRECTIONAL FACILITIES - Since you will be a Certified Minister, you can visit others in need!! Preach the Word of God to those who have strayed from the flock.

WANT TO START YOUR OWN CHURCH?? After your LEGAL ORDINATION, you may start your own congregation!!

At this point you must be wondering how much the Certificate costs. Right? Well, let's talk about how much the program is worth. Considering the value of becoming a CERTIFIED MINISTER I'd say the program is easily worth $100. Wouldn't you agree? However, it won't cost that much. Not even close! My goal is to make this life changing program affordable so average folks can benefit from the power of it. Since I know how much you want to help others, you're going to receive your Minister Certification for under $100.00... Not even $50.00... You are going to receive the entire life-changing course for only $29.95."

Imagine that. For just $29.95 I could legally marry my sister. Of course I think my wife and/or my brother-in-law might have something to say about that, not to mention what my sister would say. As for marrying my best man, I like the guy, but he just isn't my type.

I can't think of anyone who would want to have me officiate at a funeral. Remember, I'm the guy who wants to have a motion detector attached to a tape recorder hidden inside my coffin so that I can share a few words with anyone who approaches it during the funeral.

Some people wouldn't want the minister trying to put the f-u-n in their Aunt Zelda's funeral.

I could really enjoy forgiving sins. Of course I might have a few less orthodox penances to hand out in return for my blessed intercession with the Big Guy. I think a lot of them would involve standing naked on the city hall steps singing the Oscar Meyer Weiner song.

I don't think I'd be all that interested in visiting prisons. I had too many teachers who predicted that I'd probably end up in one someday and I don't want to let them be right, even if it's just on a technicality.

Starting my own church, though... Now that could be interesting. I wonder if it could be one of those TV churches where I get to beg for money in return for my ministrations. Maybe I could even start my own university and start giving out degrees in theology. Of course, now that Minister Charles Simpson has set the price bar at $29.95, I'd have to sell an awful lot of them to make the payments on a Cadillac.

I showed one of the emails to a friend of mine who just happens to be a real, live, honest-to-goodness, minister. She said a word that I didn't think ministers were supposed to use. I guess she could be forgiven though. After all I'm sure it must be frustrating to discover that, after she spent eight years going to university to become a minister, she could get the same credentials by just sending in a check for $29.95.

Of course, to be truly forgiven she had better know all the words to the Oscar Meyer Weiner song.

Whistling The Wrong Tune With Me

The phone rang while I was having lunch the other day. Of course it did. If the phone is going to ring around here it is bound to be at a mealtime. Most of the time it's people wanting to sell me lawn care services, duct cleaning, or a new long distance telephone-calling plan. Since I live in an apartment condominium I don't have much use for the first two, and the people selling the latter don't seem to get the idea that I am happy with my current service, despite telling them that at least once a week.

This caller was an acquaintance who thought I would be interested in joining him in a telephone campaign against Canadian Pacific Railways. Apparently he doesn't like train whistles and he would like the CPR to stop blowing theirs. He wanted me to start calling the train company's office to complain about the whistles.

The thing is I don't even hear them.

Trains started rolling along the section of track that runs through our little town in 1885. Even though my math isn't the greatest, I can still figure out that it was a long time before the caller or I ever thought about moving here. When you move close to a train track you can probably be pretty safe assuming that there are going to be trains rolling by from time to time.

The fact is I like train whistles. I'm a big supporter of the engineer's right to blow his whistle whenever he wants. If my car was ever stalled on the tracks, I think I would appreciate it if the engineer blew the whistle to let me know that I was going to die.

People like this always amuse me. They're the same sort of people who build a house close to an airport and then start complaining about the noise the planes make. There's another group that are often heard from around here. They are the folks who moved out to this semi-rural area from the city and then discovered that local farmers have cows that produce a byproduct that don't smell like a lavender potpourri.

We've lived in this town for almost fifteen years. Our first house here was only about 150 feet from the tracks. We were close enough that our house shook when a heavy grain-laden train rolled past. That was actually a benefit. When guests would come from other parts of the country we would tell them that the shaking wasn't really anything to worry too much about. It was just that our house was built on the north end of the San Andreas Fault. We got six or seven earthquakes a day.

Visitors rarely overstayed their welcome.

Our condo is now about 250 feet from the tracks. It's far enough - or maybe built well enough - that it doesn't shake when the trains roll past.

I can recall waking up in our previous home several times because of the train whistles. It wasn't really the whistle that woke me up though. It was the coyotes that spent the next fifteen minutes howling back at it. Those were the days when we shared our house with the dumbest dog to ever get lost on a single flight of stairs. The coyotes would wake her up and she'd decide that it might be a good time to get me to let her outside. I never could convince that dog that 3:30 AM wasn't my favorite time to stand in my underwear at the back door to make sure she didn't get lost by the hydrangea bush.

The caller wasn't too happy that I didn't want to join in his crusade against train whistles. I could hear his wife huffing in the background and saying that I must be an awfully sound sleeper. Since he was clearly not going to be successful recruiting me, he asked me to give him the names and numbers of other people who live near the tracks. With my lunch getting colder by the minute, I just couldn't think of anyone I disliked enough to subject them to a call from this person asking them to rise up against the evils of train whistles.

It might be different if he wanted to ban something that really is bad. Broccoli leaps to mind...

Some Things Just Aren't Titillating

I'm all for freedom of expression. I just wish some people wouldn't express themselves so visibly.

Or so often.

Our little town has a notorious citizen who feels that it is her job to keep the rest of us abreast of her opinions. If it were political opinions she was expressing I wouldn't mind. If she wanted to comment on the sorry state of our local roads, the price of gas, or the amount of tax on a case of beer I'd cheer her on without a moment's hesitation.

I think her whole cause is a bit of a bust. She wants the right to ride her bicycle through the town wearing nothing but a pair of shorts and a smile.

You'd have to be some kind of a boob to go along with her.

Don't get me wrong. I'm as red-blooded a male as the next guy. Testosterone flows through my veins too. Frankly, if Pamela Anderson wanted to ride a bike through town wearing the same shorts and smile, I'd be there to cheer her on. Unfortunately, our bare-chested rider is not doing it to show the world her wonderful body or the artistry that can be attributed to her favorite plastic surgeon.

I think she may be doing it to scare small children and dogs.

It works.

As Jeff Foxworthy says, whenever you start wondering what a man is thinking, odds are it has something to do with wanting a beer and wanting to see something naked. I had the unfortunate experience to seeing our half-naked bicyclist recently. I don't know how many beers it is going to take to get the image out of my mind, but I don't plan on stopping until amnesia sets in. Just writing about it is enough to send me into one of those whole-body quivers.

This particular woman also feels it's her right to show up at the town swimming pool in similar attire, or rather lack thereof. Thankfully I haven't witnessed her version of the breaststroke. Those who have say that it has the same effect on pool patrons as seeing a shark's dorsal fin has on Florida beach swimmers.

I'm not trying to be some kind of moralist here. I think that people have every right to their nudity, but some people should remember that their right to show off acres of bare flesh ends where my right not to be ill starts. Some simple rules should be followed to protect the innocent, the guilty and me.

For example:

- If you look down and cannot see your feet for your stomach, you shouldn't ride a bicycle naked.
- If your birthday suit looks like it is need of a good ironing, you shouldn't ride a bicycle naked.
- If you had to buy a new belt because your old one was pinching your nipples, you shouldn't ride a bicycle naked.
- And perhaps, most importantly, if the hummingbird you had tattooed on your left breast when you were younger now looks more like a turkey vulture, you shouldn't ride a bicycle naked.

I know that there are those who will say that I am supporting some sort of double standard because men can ride bicycles without wearing a shirt. I think I'm on fairly safe ground in my degree of chauvinism here.

It should be tit for tat.

Men should have to live by the same set of rules when it comes to exposing themselves in public. That's just one of the many reasons why you will never see me riding a bicycle without wearing a shirt. I lost visual contact with my toes years ago. My birthday suit looks like I've slept in it for nearly fifty years. While I don't have a tattoo, the surgical scar that was the size of an earthworm in 1978 now looks more like an anaconda.

I think I should be commended for the public service I provide by keeping all of that safely hidden by a golf shirt.

...and it's a very big golf shirt.

Not All Air-
Terrorist Weapons Go Boom

While flying is not one of my favorite pastimes, I'm not really afraid to do it. I know some people who are downright terrified at the prospect of getting into an aircraft. Sitting in a few dozen tons of metal and believing that it will stay 30,000 feet in the air doesn't really give me a problem.

It's the other passengers.

They scare the heck out of me.

Let's face it. For the last few years we've all had the same thought every time we've boarded an aircraft. Whether it's sitting at the gate or watching the other passengers walk toward you down the aisle of the plane, we've all played our own version of Spot The Terrorist.

Naturally, we all have our own ideas about what a terrorist looks like. Racial profiling aside, I have several clues that I look for when trying to determine the potential threat posed by any of my fellow passengers. In the four flights that I've made in the last two weeks, I've been convinced that terrorists accompanied me on every single one of them.

Probably the terrorist that causes the greatest amount of fear to go through my system is the one who enters the aircraft carrying an innocuous looking bundle. It's too big to be a box cutter, too lumpy to be an M-16, and it's squirming too much to be a bomb.

I always find it amazing that people can actually get these things past security because there is no single greater threat to air passengers than babies and small children.

I've seen these little living weapons of mass destruction cause all kinds of havoc on a flight. There are the ones who scream through five-hour, cross-country trips only to fall asleep as we start the final approach to the airport at our destination. Worse still, are the ones who can launch the contents of their stomachs from a point mid-way through economy all the way up to first class.

You'd think the least the mother could do is shout, "Incoming!" after her little darling fires, so that the victims have a little warning before being hit by a BPG (baby propelled glop.)

Sometimes terrorists bring on mobile versions of these weapons. Oh, the on-board destruction a toddler can inflict. I've seen small arms reach over seatbacks and pull toupees off of victims' heads. I've had more than one discover that I am not wearing a toupee but still try to significantly reduce my hair follicle count.

The most spectacular example of onboard terrorism that I have witnessed involved a small child running up and down the aisle with a bottle filled with a liquid solution that combined water, sugar, and large amounts of red food dye. When the child tripped the bottle was launched. It struck the overhead bins causing the top to blow off, emptying the contents over three rows of passengers, saving the greatest amount of liquid for the keyboard of a businessman's laptop.

It made the strangest sound just before the screen went blank. The businessman made a strange sound too.

Another form of terrorist doesn't wreck havoc while the plane is in the air. They attack at the gate. Their weapons are hidden inside backpacks. Their victims are anyone seated in an aisle seat before they board or still sitting there when they rush for the door at the destination.

I sit on the aisle. Because I walk on crutches, I pre-board the aircraft and I wait until the other passengers have left before getting off. As a result I am a sitting duck.

For some reason, people wearing backpacks are oblivious to the fact that it sticks out a foot and a half behind them. When they reach their seat they make a right angle turn. The backpack bludgeons anyone sitting close by.

When the French designed the Airbus line of passenger aircraft, they included a terrorist weapon in every seat. While all aircraft seats have that little button to raise and lower the seatback, the Airbus seats are closer to one another than in other aircraft I've flown. Therefore, if the passenger in front of you tries to recline their seat, you are likely to suffer a variety of contusions.

On a flight last week from Detroit to Denver I sat beside a man who could have hired Shaquille O'Neal to portray his Mini-Me.

A geriatric terrorist in the seat ahead of me tried to recline her seat. My knees were pressed firmly against it preventing any movement. Undeterred she repeated the maneuver.

Again, and again, and again...

I think she must have been hoping that my legs might shrink during the flight. Finally, in a last ditch effort, the terrorist leaned forward and gave her seatback an almighty shove. My left knee was propelled into the rock-hard thigh of the sleeping Shaq-alike, and the right one was pushed into the beverage cart in the aisle. Both the Shaqclone and the flight attendant looked at me as though the whole thing was my idea of a fun way to pass the time on a long flight.

And if the thought of being repositioned in my seat by a groggy giant and a ticked off flight attendant isn't airline terror I just don't know what is.

Is That Woman Singing, Or Did Someone Set Fire To Her Toenails?

Technology has brought us many things that I really wouldn't know what to do without, now that I have gotten used to having them to complain about. I can't imagine life without the automatic teller machine, the pay-at-the-pump self-serve gas station, or the easy accessibility of e-mail.

Without those things we might be reduced to actually interacting with another human being on a one-to-one basis every now and then.

To hear my sons speak, it's a wonder their mother or I survived the prehistoric days before technology came to our rescue with calculators, home computers and microwave ovens. They cannot imagine the hardships we faced, actually having to wait while something cooked in a conventional oven. In their minds we might just as well have been living in a cave somewhere, cooking our meals over an open fire.

They cannot comprehend sitting down and writing a letter to someone with anything as antiquated as a pen. For that matter why just limit our conversations to one person over a telephone when we could be talking to dozens at once in a chat room. It's always with a mixture of pity and distain whenever they talk about the old days - you know, before the invention of the Pentium chip.

I have to admit that I've embraced much of what technology has wrought over the last few years. I spend much of my day working at, and frequently swearing at, a computer. The Internet lets me get my column out to newspapers with just the push of a button. When I first started writing this column, most of the newspapers couldn't accept a column by e-mail. I was left to the whims of the post office, or dealing with horrific long distance telephone bills resulting from sending the column out by fax.

Despite what my sons might believe, I have never been reduced to chiseling out a column on a slab of rock, or painting one in hieroglyphics on a cave wall.

Like anything else, technology can be put to good use, or it can be used to cause pain. I encountered the perfect example to back up that statement just yesterday.

We've all become used to sitting on hold, while waiting for "the next available customer service representative" to stop filing her nails, defending his lead in a video game, or whatever it is that customer service representatives do while we dutifully sit at the other end of the line waiting for them to grant us an audience.

Today's corporate telephone systems use technology to inflict some form of nondescript music upon us while we wait.

I don't have a problem with that. I can listen to country-on-hold, classical-on-hold, rock-on-hold, or advertising jingles-on-hold without developing even the slightest hint of aggravation. I could probably even be content to wait for the elusive next available customer service representative while listening to Tibetan monks chanting the lyrics to *We All Live In A Yellow Submarine,* but what I experienced while on hold for my long-distance provider yesterday was downright inhumane.

There should be laws prohibiting cruel and unusual punishment of this nature. Greenpeace would undoubtedly protest if someone made whales listen to it. The A.C.L.U. would sue if condemned prisoners were subjected to it while they wait for the electricity to hit their chair.

It sounded like someone running fingernails down a chalkboard set to music.

That's right; I had to listen to opera-on-hold.

The woman singing sounded like she had ignored the warning on her electric curling iron that says you aren't supposed to use it internally. When I tried to protect my future ability to hear by holding the receiver away from my ears, the dog ran from the room. I think she may have been the only one who could hear some of the notes the singer was reaching.

When, at long last, the next available customer service representative rescued me, I pointed out that their choice of on-hold music left something to be desired. He said that many of their customers found it relaxing. These are, I assume, the same people who can relax while a mugging, rape, or gangland execution takes place under their apartment windows.

I realize that there are people who enjoy listening to the proverbial fat lady squawk at the top of her lungs in an indeterminate language. They will defend operatic caterwauling as a great art form. I can accept their right to listen to it, even if I don't understand the attraction. I'm not saying that there is anything wrong with these people...

...but I bet they like broccoli too.

Oh What A Strange Web We Weave

I get a lot of emails. Actually it's not really a lot. It's more like an infestation. Plagues of locusts probably have fewer entries than my email box on any given day.

I get emails telling me that I am, among other things mentally deficient, chauvinistic, sexist, and a Boomer, but those are just the ones sent by my family members. I also get sent every joke, urban myth, and plea to help raise funds for earthquake victims in Antarctica. On any given week I will receive several emails offering to share the proceeds of the estate of a deposed dictator in Africa, as well as dozens upon dozens of offers to join in the most incredible money-making business opportunity to see the light of day since last week.

I also receive a lot of emails from people who would like me to visit their website or who have somehow stumbled upon a website that is, to put it politely, odd. Some of them go even further, beyond odd, to a place where words escape me. I thought I would share a few of these with you.

People who do not want to stop at putting one of those chrome fish symbols on their car, can now share their religious zeal with the entire neighborhood. A British company offers an inflatable church for your backyard, complete with a 57-foot high steeple, stained glass windows, and an inflatable pulpit. I visited the company's website at http://www.inflatablechurch.com. It extols the benefits of owning or renting an inflatable church, and points out that its hard floor even allows worshipers to enter wearing high heels.

They do suggest that parishioners refrain from smoking. I suppose an accidentally dropped butt could blow the whole thing to someplace that churches are not normally associated with.

You can also watch a video on the website complete with a British minister who looks like he may have been inflated too. Just for that special added effect, they have the London Gay Men's Choir singing a Christmas carol thrown in for good measure.

I suppose your inflatable church could be used for funerals. Perhaps as an added feature you might offer to introduce your grieving parishioners to the website at http://www.

afterlifetelegrams.com. For a fee of $10 per word (and a five-word minimum) the folks running this website will deliver a message to someone who has left this life. According to the information on the site, this is done with the help of terminally Ill volunteers who memorize the telegrams before passing away, and then deliver the telegrams when they reach the great hereafter.

Let's see, at $10 per word I could send, "Dad, can I borrow a hundred to pay for this."

We've all seen supposed psychics bend cutlery with their minds. Personally I could never really see the use for such a skill. I can drop food from my fork onto a clean shirt quite easily without it being all bent out of shape. If, however, you are one of those people who would like to amaze and astonish your friends, step-by-step instruction in the art of cutlery mangling can be found at http://www.fork-you.com. Just make sure you spell that correctly or you could end up in a much different sort of website.

Clearly some people have a lot of time on their hands. The folks who run http://www.mycathatesyou.com have filled a website with cats making unpleasant faces at the camera. Many of them seem strikingly similar to the faces I make whenever I have to walk past our cat's litter box.

OK, so who among us would be surprised to learn that California is home to one of the more unusual festivities detailed on a website. Visit http://www.moonamtrak.org/ to learn all the details needed to attend the Annual Mooning Of Amtrak in Laguna Niguel, California. During the day twenty Amtrak passenger trains pass by the gathering of mooners. In addition there are another four opportunities for night mooning. The organizers recommend bringing a powerful flashlight or camping lantern to give the Amtrak passengers the full moon effect.

Of course, if it's true weirdness you want, why go any further than my column. I have recently been installed in my own private padded cell in cyberspace at http://www.gordonkirkland.com. Those of you who are much more computer literate than I am will already know that I have been stuck in traffic on the information cul-de-sac for years.

I promise that there will never be any photos of me participating in the Mooning of Amtrak.

I Don't Have An Accent, But You Sure Do, Eh?

I was watching the news reports of the Australian brush fires a few days ago. I realize that brush fires might be a bit of an unusual start for a humor column, but then most of my readers don't expect usual things from me anyway.

Obviously brush fires aren't funny. What caught my attention though were the accents of the people describing the scenes of burning trees and homes, and that got me thinking. (Yes, dear readers, every so often when the moon is in the right orbit I actually do think.) I started to wonder why, when we supposedly speak the same language, we find so many ways to pronounce the same words.

It reminded me of a story I read a few years ago about an Australian hospital that decided to send all of their doctors and nurses to diction lessons. Apparently more than one of them has caused a high degree of stress in their patients when they have said, "You can go home today." Unfortunately, that particular phrase, when said with an Australian accent sounds more like, "You can go home to die."

As a Canadian who spends a lot of time in the United States I get my share of teasing about the way I say certain words and phrases. Words like 'out' and 'about' apparently sound like 'oot' and 'aboot' when a Canadian speaks them and an American hears them.

Part way through a radio interview in Nashville a few years ago the host stopped me and said, "Say 'hawuss' again."

"Do you mean house?" I asked.

"Yeah," he said. "Say it in Canadian again."

Naturally, one of the things that Americans tend to notice about Canadians speech patterns is our tendency to end sentences, with "eh?" as in; "It sure is cold oot and aboot today, eh?"

Americans on the other hand often end sentences with "huh?" It's the same thing, just a different choice of meaningless word. Actually, both sounds can convey a lot of information, thereby conserving energy for other more important activities. For example, an American and a Canadian could watch a baseball game together and communicate with nothing but those two sounds, thereby saving valuable time for beer drinking and snack food eating.

Sammy Sosa hitting a home run would result in the conversation sounding like:

"Huh!"

"Eh!"

A bad call from the umpire would result in:

"Huh?"

"Eh?"

Let's not even get started on the way people talk in the Deep South. I'm still in trouble with my wife for my response to a waitress who offered me "a piece of ass" for my soda. Apparently she was talking about a cube of frozen water.

Even within the same boundaries we can say things a lot differently. The name of that big city in Michigan where they make cars is a constant point of contention around my house. I grew up in Toronto and have always pronounced it "Dee-troy-it." My wife, who grew up about four hundred miles to the west, just across the river from Dee-troy-it, pronounces it "Detroyt."

Over the years my pronunciation of that city's name has become one of my wife's biggest pet peeves about me. It falls somewhere in between missing the laundry basket with my socks and leaving dirty dishes in the living room.

Naturally I take this into consideration and try to work as many references to the Dee-troy-it Red Wings hockey team as possible into our conversations. Of course, deep down, I know that am the one who is incorrect. It isn't so much because of the way I pronounce it, but because it is me doing the pronouncing. To paraphrase something that I have said before, if a man says Dee-troy-it in a forest with no around to hear him he will still be wrong.

There doesn't even have to be too great a distance to produce multiple ways of pronouncing the same thing. I did an appearance in Louisville, Kentucky a few years ago. Over the course of a couple days I think I heard twenty-seven different ways of saying Louisville - all from people who lived there.

Let's face it. It doesn't really matter how we pronounce the words we use as long as we can understand most of what the other people are saying. Of course there are exceptions. Obviously, those Australian doctors should be a bit more careful.

...and I'd be thankful if waitresses in the Deep South would learn how to say 'ice,' eh?

It's A Fact. I'm Flooded With Facts.

In among the flotsam and jetsam that cross my desk each week is the occasional little bit of information that makes me stop and wonder about the complexities of life on Earth. The rest just makes me stop and wonder why someone thought I needed to know the information that they sent me.

Someone at the University of California, Davis faxed me a press release last week to tell me that young musicians are invited to a summer camp at the University of California, Davis. While I may have made a conscious decision to avoid growing up, I don't think I fit in the "young" category any more. My musical abilities are largely limited to playing a mean rendition of In-A-Gadda-Da-Vida on the kazoo. Then there's the small point that I don't live anywhere near Davis, California.

On a single day last year I received a total of seventeen faxes to let me know that Tipper Gore was moderating a mental health awareness campaign. Perhaps someone was trying to tell me something. It may be some sort of strange synchronicity but those faxes all arrived the same week that one of Mrs. Gore's relatives spilled red wine on my brother's Persian rug. Maybe those faxes should have been going to Jim to help him deal with the posttraumatic stress of seeing the wine hit the rug.

"It looked like it went in slow motion," he said, "especially the part where my wife was trying to catch it before it hit the rug."

Email has created an overload of information coming my way each day. If I were to print every email that gets inserted into my computer I would expect to see Greenpeace activists picketing outside my front door for my part in the destruction of a couple of million trees. Often, when an email filled with useless facts arrives from one person, it means that I can expect to receive identical copies of it from a couple of hundred other people. One such email makes an appearance every few weeks. It's filled with information that a lot of people seem determined to add to my knowledge base. Some of it is interesting. Some of it is unbelievable.

Obviously, it's something I need to share with you.

Did you know, or for that matter, did you ever have the slightest interest in knowing, that elephants are the only animals that cannot jump? I'm not sure why, but I find that little bit of information comforting. I can rest assured that I will never be crushed by a random act of pacaderm hopscotch.

I don't find it particularly interesting that all polar bears are left-handed. I do have to wonder how that bit of knowledge came about though. Has someone actually surveyed the population of polar bears to see which paw they prefer to use to disembowel seals and polar bear researchers?

I wonder if it was the same government grant that paid someone to determine that crocodiles cannot stick out their tongues. I'm sure if they could they would love to make that little unspoken statement to the Australian guy who keeps jumping on top of them and shouting, "Crikey! Ain't she a beauty?"

There is one fact in the email that always amuses me. Apparently it is impossible to lick your own elbow.

Now that's the kind of information that the world needs to know isn't it? How often have you felt like licking your elbow and wondered why you just can't quite reach it with your tongue? Now you know the futility of trying again. My dog on the other paw, is quite adept a licking what would be her elbow. She's also capable of licking several other places that humans would find extremely difficult and she shows off that skill whenever we have company.

I've often written about my heightened state of nervousness whenever I have to fly. The events of the few couple of years haven't done much to ease those feelings. Still, thanks to the information provided in the fact-filled email, I can now get on a plane with the knowledge that fewer people are killed in airplane crashes than in donkey attacks each year.

Another frequent note that crosses my desk lists a number of stellar points about being Canadian. For example, all Canadians should be proud that they live in the country with the largest population of French speaking people who have never surrendered to Germany.

I'm sure that most of you would agree that all of this information is pretty useless. Still, I would really like to know how many of you stopped part way through this story and tried to try to lick your elbows.

I'm Just Not Jumpy

Every year, as the temperatures start to rise and the days get longer, a group of people descends on the small town I call home. These people are just not quite normal and I am always a bit concerned when I see them. One thing is for sure. You can't stop them once they start.

Some towns get tourists. Some are even lucky enough to get motorcycle gangs. Not my town. We get people who jump out of airplanes a couple of thousand feet over our peaceful little village. Oh sure, they have parachutes, but I cannot fathom why someone would prefer to get to the ground dangling under a piece of cloth, when they could wait a few minutes and let the pilot bring them to a safe landing at the airport.

I've written before about how flying is not one of my favorite things. Actually the flying isn't so bad. It's the taking off and landing that gets to me. It seems if you are going to become intimately familiar with the logistics of an airplane crash, it's going to be either when you are taking off or landing.

Even so, I would much rather stay on board the plane until it had finished its flight than to step out for some fresh air before the pilot has brought the plane to a complete halt and turned off the seatbelt lights.

It's also one of the reasons that I am glad that I no longer smoke. On a recent flight, the flight attendant announced that anyone caught smoking during the flight would be asked to leave immediately. I bet it's hard to keep a cigarette lit after stepping through the door of an airplane at 36,000 feet.

The Pitt Meadows International Airport and Chinese Restaurant is home to a few small planes, a couple of helicopters, and a whole collection of these people who try their best to be death defying. They fly an ancient plane that holds about ten of them at a time. We hear the plane's engines as it circles overhead trying to gain enough altitude for the jumpers to go through their out-of-aircraft routine. If I was the jumper I can imagine just what that routine might entail:

1. Losing what remains of my sanity and stepping through the plane's door.

2. Spending a few minutes trying to remember why I took step one.
3. Realizing that step two is causing me to use up most of the space between the plane door and the ground.
4. Trying to remember which ring opens the parachute and which one undoes the straps holding it on my back.
5. Realizing that step four has used up even more of the space between the plane and a fatal splat.
6. Remembering which ring to pull and opening my parachute.
7. Realizing that it would have been better if I had been looking at the ground when I pulled the ring so that the parachute would have opened over me, not under me.
8. Coming to the very real conclusion that my jump suit was going to need a thorough cleaning.
9. Finally discovering that falling several thousand feet isn't painful at all.
10. Discovering that hitting the ground is.

It's illegal if a drug dealer offers a sample of his wares. People get concerned if a cult invites people to come and try out their brand of thinking. Apparently it isn't nearly as big a reason for alarm if parachute clubs try to get people to try out their brand of excitement. They even have a great big sign in town offering parachuting lessons. Oh sure, I've looked at that sign and wondered what it might be like to feel the impact of the wind in my face several thousand feet above my house. I usually dispel that thought by realizing that I have no real desire to feel the impact of the shingles that are, for all intents and purposes, zero feet above my house.

I know that some of you will take this column as an indication that I am a fearful person, unwilling to face dangers. I want to make it perfectly clear that I am quite willing to laugh in the face of a wide variety of dangerous situations.

Just the other day I admitted to my wife that I had mixed lights and darks in the washing machine. If that isn't danger, then I just don't know what is.

I have been a passenger in a car driven by my son while he was still learning to drive. Danger must be my middle name.

I have even called upon my deepest reserves of courage and actually put broccoli in my mouth, chewed it and swallowed it.

Believe me. That takes courage.

Section Six:
The World As I See It Is An Odd Little Place

When My Mind Wanders It Brings Back Souvenirs

Gonna Get Me My Kind Of Gun

While I'm not a big fan of guns, and I don't think Charlton Heston and I would ever see eye to eye on the need for attack weapons when duck hunting, I do see that there is a place in this world for guns.

For example, if I am ever surrounded by a pack of rabid dogs, I hope someone comes along with a gun to prevent me from having to go through anti-rabies injections.

...again.

If I am ever on an airplane with someone who tries to set off a plastic explosive by holding a match to his shoe, I'd be pretty relieved if the stewardess was packing more than just little bottles of scotch in her beverage cart.

I have never owned a gun of any kind. Oh, sure, I've shot guns a few times, but I've always had an undeniable urge to check my underwear every time I pull a trigger. Still, my heart beat a little faster when I saw a new automatic weapon described on the front page of the newspaper the other day. Oh, what a joy it would be to own such a thing of beauty.

I want one.

I really, really want one.

It looks like one of those Gatling guns we've all seen in the old war movies. It's mounted on a tripod, and its stock is made from beautifully sanded wood. Its magazine held 144 rounds that could be fired as fast as the user could turn the crank.

Not bullets.

Rubber bands.

Over the years I have developed a certain proficiency with rubber bands. Like many people, when it comes to learning how to handle a weapon, I was taught by my father, who showed me that it was possible to make my mother throw a paperback book over her head if you could quietly take aim and hit the back of the book while she was engrossed in the story. I also learned that my father didn't think it was nearly as funny when I practiced my shot by letting loose with a large rubber band into the back page of the newspaper he was reading. For some reason, my wife never sees the humor in that either.

I was once locked in a prolonged rubber band war when I worked for a large, multinational accounting and consulting firm. A colleague and I worked closely together on our projects and were pretty much left to our own devices by the rest of the five hundred or so people in the office. At times, the workload and the stress of maintaining our client billings would build to the point where it desperately needed to be released.

It was one of those times that my colleague decided to declare war on me.

I was sitting at my desk, with my back to the door, pouring over a ream of computer printouts detailing something scintillating like the national statistics on personal bankruptcy. When the first elastic band hit the computer printout from over my shoulder, I thought I was going to have to go home and change my suit.

If it was war he wanted, it was war he was going to get.

Over the next six months neither of us was safe at our desks. I rearranged my office so that I would face the door, but he still managed to get in a couple of good shots each day. Not to be outdone, I took great pleasure in my stealth rubber band attacks on him. No one in the office was truly safe. An innocent bystander would occasionally get caught in the crossfire.

I knew I was defeated when he launched his secret weapon - the rubber band time bomb. He snuck into my office one day and hung a long rubber band from the pin holding a calendar on my wall. He hooked my umbrella into the rubber band and left it dangling, thinking that it would eventually fall to the floor and scare the living crap out of me once and for all.

It worked better than he could ever have imagined.

Not only did the umbrella crash to the floor, it pulled the pin from the wall and sent it flying towards my turned back. I'm not sure what startled me more; the crash of the umbrella, or the pin passing through my hair just before it hit the wall in front of me.

He may have won that war, but if I can come up with a spare $395.00 for a 144-round rubber band machine gun, I'm going to hunt him down and claim victory for myself.

My cause is just. I will prevail.

I'm Learning Every Day...
Bless My Heart

It has been said that we must continue learning throughout out lives to keep our minds alert. Being on tour is a great education.

I'm just not sure how alert my mind is.

On this trip, for example, I have learned that no matter how hard you try to plan your flights, outside forces can mess that up in a heartbeat. In this case, heavy rain, hail and tornadoes in the Denver area prevented my plane from landing there. Instead, we did a figure-eight over Idaho Falls for close to an hour, until our fuel ran low. We then flew to Billings, Montana to refuel.

I hadn't planned on landing in Billings, Montana. One needs to be mentally prepared for Billings, Montana.

On the other hand, one also has to be mentally prepared for running out of fuel over Idaho Falls, so I guess Billings was the lesser of two evils.

As a result, I arrived in Georgia four hours after I planned on getting there. I didn't collapse onto my hotel bed until after 2:00 AM, which explains the aforementioned lack of mental alertness.

Still, despite my reduced capacities I was still able to learn a great deal in the three days I spent in Georgia.

For one thing, Georgians are an incredibly polite group of people.

Other writers should take note, that in Georgia if a fan of your writing wants to be your stalker, they will ask your permission first. I guess that's why Stephen King didn't set his novel, Misery, in Georgia. The movie wouldn't have been the same if Kathy Bates had to ask permission before hitting the author in the legs with a sledge hammer.

I also learned an important rule of Georgian etiquette. Apparently, one can say anything about another person, and be perfectly polite about it, as long as they end the comment with "Bless his heart" or "Bless her heart."

An example that I was given was that you could look at a woman and say something along the lines of, "She has a butt that looks like two pigs fighting in a burlap sack... bless her heart."

Can you just imagine what it would be like if that rule of etiquette spread?

For one thing, politics would never be the same.

"I think my opponent has fewer working brain cells than a gnat... bless his heart."

"My opponent has never met a decision that he couldn't take both sides of... bless his heart."

"The men in that other party are a bunch of girly boys... bless their hearts."

I can only imagine what the whispered conversations must be like at weddings in Georgia.

"My, those bridesmaid dresses make them look like something out of an explosion at a paint factory... bless their hearts."

"The groom is so dumb he forgot to think about how the bride's mother looks after putting on a couple of hundred pounds... bless his heart. Oh and bless the bride's mother's heart too."

"Well, would you look at that? She's actually wearing white... bless her heart."

I think I will try to bring this method of southern etiquette back home with me. Of course, I will have to fully explain it to my family, so that they know anything I say using the phrase "bless your heart" should be accepted without feeling insulted. I can already think of several ways of using it:

"When you said you were ready to get going I didn't realize that it meant that you still had to curl your hair, put on your make-up, check your email, and rearrange the living room furniture... bless your heart."

"Son, you've eaten an entire package of forty-eight cheese slices in just three days... bless your heart."

"That building council in our condo makes rules for other people, but not the council members... bless their hearts."

"That bookstore owner who forgot to order enough copies of my book ahead of my appearance has the business sense of a slug... bless her heart."

"I planned my own flights again... bless my heart."

I Know The Important Stuff About My Car - It's Green

I have to say from the outset that I really like my car.

Most guys like their cars. Some have stronger feelings about their cars than they do about their families. Some even understand their cars better than they understand their families.

I am not one of those guys, not that I've ever claimed to understand my family that well, either.

I have a very limited understanding about my car. I put gas in the back, I put the keys in the ignition, and I expect it to do the rest. I don't really care how it does all of the other things it is supposed to do, just as long as it does it.

I feel pretty much the same way about my digestive tract.

My car isn't a classic, but it isn't particularly new, either. It's a 1997 Pontiac Grand Am GT. When I saw it on the lot, I knew it was the car I wanted. I didn't have to kick the tires, look under the hood, or even take it for a test drive.

It was green.

It had a sunroof.

It had a CD player.

It had a little door at the back that told me where to put the gas. It had a spot to put the keys to make it start.

Let's face it; it was everything I could ever want, all rolled up in a nice looking package.

A few months ago, I received a recall notice for the car. I called the dealership. The service manager asked if the car had a specific feature. From what I recall it sounded like he asked if the car came equipped with a dual circulating instep with chrome rotating bivalve a-la-mode semi-wankers.

"It's green," I told him.

He tried to simplify his question, "Under the hood is there a chrome thing that looks like an upside-down miniature hockey stick?

"It has a sunroof," I added, "and a CD player."

There was a clearly audible sigh from the other end of the phone. I've heard that sigh from a lot of mechanics.

I decided it would probably be best if I just took the car in to the guys who do all the other work on my car. At least John and Jeff know that I have no idea what goes on after the gas goes in through that little door in the back and I turn the key. They don't judge me for my lack of mechanical abilities.

At least not to my face.

They know that I understand the really important things about my car. It's green. It has a sunroof. It has a CD player. And most importantly, I know that it is best if I pay them to know about all the other stuff.

They seem to like that last part.

My car insurance was due a few days ago. I dutifully took the car in to the anti-pollution agency be tested, as required before I could reinsure it.

It failed.

How could my car fail? After all, didn't the tester notice that it was green, with a sunroof and a CD player?

Apparently, its exhaust has too many hydrocarbons. I think my dog has the same problem fairly frequently.

I took the car to see John and Jeff. I was sure it was going to be something simple. The CD player probably needed adjusting. Maybe I should have shut the sunroof during the test because the dog was in the back seat.

Jeff gave me the bad news; the eight-hundred-dollar bad news.

Apparently my catalytic converter wasn't converting my catalytics anymore. I didn't even know that I had catalytics, much less that they needed to be converted. Frankly, if catalytics don't knock on my door and try to convert me, I won't try to convert them. In addition, some sensors were no longer sensing.

Since I am going to be away from home on tour so much of the next few months, I decided to store the car until I would have more need of it in the fall, and forget about its hydrocarbons, catalytics and its dual circulating instep with chrome rotating bivalve a-la-mode semi-wankers.

I can still enjoy the car when I go for a visit. It's still green, has a sunroof, and a CD player.

When you've got all that, who needs it to move?

Signs You Are In The South

I have just gotten home from almost three weeks on the road, most of it in southern states like Georgia, Alabama and Tennessee. It may take me a while to get my Canadian accent back.

I start each day standing in front of my mirror repeating "out and about," going for more of an "owt and abowt" than an 'at and abat.' I'm trying to get the word 'eh' back at the end of my sentences. It's a bit more difficult dropping the extra syllables in monosyllabic words and refraining from saying y'all and all y'all.

I think I may need to have a few more Canadian brands of beer to get my vocabulary retuned perfectly. At least that's going to be my excuse, eh.

I managed to put nearly three thousand miles on my rental car during the trip. A lot of it was spent on interstates, but from time to time I took the roads less traveled.

Perhaps it was the signs along the way that caught my attention more than anything else. I saw signs that would have directed me to some oddly named landmarks had I not been past them before their words fully sank in.

For example, just a few miles south of the Ohio River there is sign directing tourists to an oddly named state park. I have no idea how it got its name, and frankly, I don't think that I want to know.

You can draw your own conclusions about how they came up with the name Big Bone Lick State Park. My editors wouldn't want me to do it for you.

I drove across Kentucky on the Blue Grass Parkway through fantastic scenery. Anyone with a love for horses should take that drive. I think there may be more horses than people through that stretch of the country. As I neared the end of the Parkway I saw a sign that I knew I had to follow.

"Turn here for the Historic Maker's Mark Distillery."

I had discovered Maker's Mark bourbon a few years ago at a dinner the distillery sponsored for the National Society of Newspaper Columnists. As we entered the room we were handed a glass. Throughout the evening, the employees of Maker's Mark made sure those glasses never emptied.

I don't remember returning to my hotel.

I'm not even sure if I can remember the next day at the conference.

The drive to the distillery was along a winding narrow highway. About twenty miles from the Parkway I entered the town of Loretto, Kentucky. The town sign proclaimed it to be the home of both Maker's Mark and The Sisters of Loretto.

It must be a very happy convent.

Heading to Interstate 65 from Loretto took me though several towns that I could not even find on the official Kentucky road map. One of them had a sign that I had to turn back to make sure I had read correctly. If any of my readers can explain the sign I would truly appreciate hearing from you.

In large, hand painted letters it boldly proclaimed, "Enjoy Kentucky - We Don't Rent Pigs."

What the heck does that mean? Are there states where pig renting is a common practice? Does a rental pig come with an extended warranty against wolves huffing and puffing and blowing your house down?

As I neared Hodgenville, Kentucky, every sign had something to do with Abraham Lincoln.

"Visit Lincoln's Birthplace."

"See Lincoln's Boyhood Home At Knob Hill."

"Turn Here For Lincoln's First Schoolhouse."

I was half expecting to see, "Sit In Lincoln's First Privy."

Perhaps the strangest sign I saw on this trip was in Alabama. Anyone who reads the sign would never bother to call the company. Those who could use the company's services would never read the sign.

It said, "Illiterate? Call 1-800..."

I always enjoy myself when I am in the South. The concept of southern hospitality is alive and well, and I thoroughly enjoy the people I meet when I am down there. I'd never want to insinuate that things are a little different there.

But, let's face it, the signs are there.

Lost (Dignity) In Space

Space may be the final frontier where people take one small step for man in a galaxy far, far away, but after spending a day at the Kennedy Space Center, I think I will let other people take those small steps. Seeing everything about the space program up close – and at times a little too personal – took some of the luster and glamour from the life of an astronaut.

The people at the Kennedy Space Centre invited me for a visit to help with the research I am doing for an article about accessibility for the disabled at tourist destinations. They have put a lot of work into making the visitor center more accessible, and they let me try to prove it by opening the doors to the whole facility for me. I had a thoroughly enjoyable day there and found that the accessibility was better than I have found at other venues.

Despite all of that, it made me quite glad that NASA will not likely ever invite me to go for a ride into that final frontier.

TV has tried to tell us that we can travel through space in comfort and joy. Kirk, Spock, and Picard needed elevators to move from one part of their ships to another. I had a close look at the capsules that took man into space in the race to the moon. One thing was clear.

John Glen would have needed a shoehorn to move far enough to scratch his butt.

Spacecraft are not very big. A Volkswagen Beetle looks like a Hummer beside the tin cans these guys took to the moon. I've been in car pools that started to smell bad after a couple of stoplights. Can you imagine what these capsules would be like after a week or so in space?

I can only hope that they never sent up freeze dried chili for their space meals.

If the concept of long-term claustrophobia wasn't enough to put me off signing up for the astronaut program, my lunch with John Fabian certainly did. John was aboard two shuttle missions in the early Eighties, after an Air Force career that saw him pilot ninety combat missions in Viet Nam.

His description of attempting bathroom functions in space was not something NASA could use in a recruitment video.

I'll keep you from having to read the details of what can happen when a $50-million toilet malfunctions, but let's just say it wasn't something you'd want to hear while eating a desert containing chocolate chips and nuts.

I may never look at a chocolate chip or a peanut the same again.

John also said that the single onboard toilet caused another problem during the first hours of the flight. Apparently in zero gravity the water in the body moves up to the top third of the body. This, in turn, causes the brain to tell your kidneys and bladder to get rid of it. As a result, for the first few hours of every Shuttle flight there is a line-up of astronauts waiting to use the facilities.

I would imagine that it is hard to cross your legs and keep them crossed in space, so if you ever get the chance to go, grab the seat closest one to the toilet, and follow your mother's advice and go before you leave.

He also told me about the problems astronauts face with a form of motion sickness in space. Surprisingly, the people who suffer from motion sickness on Earth don't feel it in space. The ones who don't get it down here have a real problem when they get into space. NASA, like all good government agencies, had to come up with a unique name for the problem. They call it Space Adaptation Syndrome.

"Astronauts," said John, "Just call it vomiting."

See what a fun guy he is to share a meal with?

I'm not a big fan of fear. I could quite happily go through my life without ever experiencing anything remotely close to sitting on a launch pad in the final seconds before liftoff. John tried to put it into a perspective I could understand. He said that in comparison with being married for forty-two years, the fear experienced during a Shuttle liftoff was nothing.

Maybe so, but I don't think I could handle the combination.

All Work And No Leisure Can Make You Want To Swim With Sharks

I was asked to discuss what leisure time means to me the other day. I remember leisure time. Twenty-five years ago, when I was employed by the government I had a lot of leisure time – especially between the hours of 8:00 AM and 4:00 PM. Today leisure time is a bit harder to find.

Having my office in my home means I am always at work, and according to my wife, I'm also always at home.

In the hours that I should be working, I'm often distracted by a variety of things around the house. The dog wants to go for a walk. The daily horde of telephone solicitors' calls interrupt my train of thought, not that my train of thought runs on all that secure a set of tracks to begin with. Last night's pizza keeps calling my name from deep within the refrigerator.

To hear my wife speak, you'd think I spend my day relaxing around the house, walking the dog, talking to telephone solicitors, and checking to see if it really was pizza that was calling my name. She believes that on top of my work and my own personal distractions I should also be able to do a variety of household chores.

On the other hand, many of my editors think that I am sitting around here, taking the dog for a walk, talking to telephone solicitors, checking for whatever it is that is calling me from inside the refrigerator, doing the vacuuming my wife asked me to do, and changing the light bulbs that blew in the kitchen two or three months ago. It just goes to show how little some editors know about me. I firmly believe that changing light bulbs, vacuuming, and most other household chores should be left in the capable hands of people who know what they are doing. I'm quite content in my ignorance of those matters.

The reverse seems to happen in the evening. When I could be thinking about leisure time, I start thinking about the work that is sitting on my desk, just a few short steps away. The guilty feelings get augmented whenever I hear the fax machine ring, or the computer making the noise that tells me that new emails have arrived. Those distractions could mean somebody wants to give me money, and it's hard to resist the temptation to go and see if it might be true.

It hasn't been yet, but you never know...

The overall result of all of this confusion is that I don't get a whole lot of time for leisure activities. About as exciting as it gets is taking a couple of hours to watch a hockey game.

Camping is not high on my to-do list. I've never particularly enjoyed serving as a mobile buffet for every variety of biting insect on the planet. Counting the places where rain is dripping through a tent is equally low on my ideas of a good time. There is a vacant lot in the next town that is occupied by a group of homeless people. They don't seem to be enjoying the camping experience either and they are probably better at it than I would be.

Skating, jogging, rock climbing, and mountain biking were all taken out of my leisure repertoire when I broke my spine. See. Being disabled does have some advantages besides getting the good parking spots.

I thought about swimming the other day. Thankfully the thought passed fairly quickly. I hate it when my subconscious starts getting more exercise than I do. My doctor thinks I should do more swimming. I don't think it would be that great an idea these days. I'm convinced that if I ever ventured into the water a team of American and Canadian marine biologists would try to get me reunited with my pod.

It hasn't always been this way. I grew up, spending my summers immersed in water. It's a wonder that my toes and fingers didn't develop webbing and that I didn't have a set of gills forming on my neck. In those days the worst time of day was that hour I had to wait after eating before I could go in the water again. With the appetite that I have today, I find that the worst time of the day is the hour after meals that I have to wait before I start hearing things calling me from the refrigerator again.

The person who was surveying my attitudes towards leisure time asked me if there was something I have always wanted to do in terms of a leisure activity, that I've never had the opportunity to experience.

Naturally there are a lot of things I'd like to try. One that usually leaves people shaking their heads when I mention it is the desire I have to go into the ocean in one of the cages to watch sharks swimming. People seem to think that idea is the last little bit of confirmation they need to determine that I have lost my mind completely.

My wife says that she will gladly go with me, right up to the part about getting into the cage and going under water. She says she will be happy to be the one who stands on the boat throwing fish guts overboard to attract the sharks.

But she wants to make sure my insurance is paid up first.

You Never Know What - Or Who - You'll Find On An Internet Auction

I've recently made my first venture into the strange world of Internet auctions. I have to admit that there is a certain interest on my part because I collect sports memorabilia. I had heard that there were some, shall we say, "unique," items listed for sale, but even my twisted and knurled outlook on life wasn't prepared for some of them.

I think some of the things being auctioned might be sure signs of the impending fall of civilization as we know it. Somewhere the four horsemen of the apocalypse are probably saddling up because they know that it is now possible to bid on a remote control beating human heart (batteries not included) on an Internet auction. On the day I looked, the bidding had reached $9.95 for that little gem.

Two bidders were fighting it out to be the winner of the auction for absolutely nothing. OK, it wasn't the most expensive item listed on the auction site, but someone was actually selling, and had convinced people of the value of, "absolutely nothing." The bidding had started at a dollar, and when I last looked it had climbed up to a full $1.29. How many other products could give you a 29% increase in their value in just a matter of days? I thought about bidding on it because I know that I started out with nothing, but I'm not sure if I still have all of it.

Another genius was offering bags of his dryer lint for auction. I'd like to say it's surprising that it was up to $5.00 for a bag.

High technology seems to have invaded ever aspect of our lives. Apparently the old standard Whoopee-Cushion has been replaced by an electronic device that's available on an Internet auction site (current bidding at $6.99.) A wireless remote control signals the thing to make one of five separate flatulence noises. Sounds like the perfect thing for state dinners in the Bush White House. Speaking of which, someone in Washington, DC was auctioning a clock that chimes each hour with a different fart.

I'm not sure how I restrained myself from bidding on the fabulous weight control device I saw offered. I would most certainly abstain from opening the refrigerator door if it had a Jim and Tammy Faye Bakker Fridge Magnet mounted at eye level.

I've been on the receiving end of the wrath of the People for the Ethical Treatment of Animals before, but I would have to say that I would side with them on one item I saw being auctioned off. An improperly named purse called the "Lucky Bag" wasn't all that lucky for its previous owner. The handbag, with a soft, leather feel was made from a kangaroo's scrotum. No stitching was required. Somehow I don't see myself being secure enough in my masculinity to bid $10.99 to try to buy my wife a scrotum big enough to hold all her change, keys, pens, gas receipts, and whatever else she keeps in her purse.

Naturally I stayed out of the section labeled "Mature Audiences." As my wife will gladly tell you I may be getting older, but I will probably never be mature.

I did discover something while looking through the auctions. On one item the current high bidder was someone named Rob Naylor. I found that strange because my best friend in the eighth grade had that very same name. Though I hate to admit it, the eighth grade was more than thirty-five years ago. We had both moved away from the small town in Ontario where we lived in 1967, and had lost contact with one another after that.

Through the power of email, I discovered that this was indeed the same Rob Naylor. Well, OK, maybe he isn't the exactly the same, after all he is thirty-some years older. I guess I've changed a bit since I was 13 too. My hair wasn't gray and my beard wasn't nearly as thick back then.

It turns out that even after three and a half decades we still share the same interests, and we even remember which girls were hot and which ones weren't, at least from the standpoint of what we considered hot in our 13-year-old minds. We remember teachers we liked, and a few that we drove to distraction.

I have to wonder though, if he might be secure enough in his masculinity to buy his wife a kangaroo scrotum handbag?

The Only Good Gopher Is A Dead Gopher – In A Tuxedo

Curiosity may have killed the cat, but it provides me with some strange column material.

Part of my appearance tour last week took me to Three Hills, Alberta, Canada to do a Writer-In-The-Schools program. Three Hills gets its name from two lumps and a mound just north of the town. In all that flatness I guess even the tiniest of clumps of dirt could be called a hill. Frankly, I've seen taller manure piles, but let's not burst their bubble. If the people there want to call them hills, I'll go along with it just to be polite.

Three Hills is northeast of Calgary. When I turned off the highway to head into the prairie in search of the town I saw the sign that spurred my curiosity. Where else but in the middle of farming country would someone erect The Gopher Hole Museum? Actually, according to the sign, it was the "World Famous Gopher Hole Museum." I must have been unconscious on the day it became world famous because I missed the news.

Still, something about that name ignited a burning desire within me to pay a visit to the Gopher Hole Museum. It raised just too many questions in my mind. Was this the site of the world's largest gopher hole? Did a backhoe operator unearth a giant prehistoric gopher somewhere around here? Do Albertans really get excited enough about gopher holes to put them on display? There seemed to be plenty of them in the fields along the road that they could look at for free, so why have a special shrine to gopher holes that charges a $2.00 admission?

It turned out that the name was a bit deceiving. The World Famous Gopher Hole Museum doesn't have any gopher holes at all. It does have gophers though – over 70 of them. Actually, they are all former gophers. The displays house stuffed gophers dressed in human clothes. They have produced over 40 scenes of daily life using dead stuffed gophers to play the parts of the humans who might normally be doing the depicted activities.

The church scene depicts a gopher preacher, with a sleeping member of the congregation and a somehow fitting, angelic gopher flying overhead. Another display has a stuffed gopher groom with his blushing gopher bride. There are Gopher fishermen, gopher bank robbers, a gopher beautician working on a blonde gopher's coiffeur, gopher cowboys and gopher Indians. There's a gopher on a camping trip, and what would a dead gopher museum in Canada be without a gopher hockey player and a gopher curler?

Perhaps the highlight was the tuxedo-clad gopher that sang, "Puttin' On The Ritz."

One thought kept running through my mind while viewing the displays. It was a quote from comedian Jeff Foxworthy, who said, "If your taxidermy bill is higher than your annual income, you might be a redneck."

Apparently the curators' claim that the museum is world famous has some merit. A few years ago those fun folks from PETA, the People For The Ethical Treatment of Animals, discovered the Gopher Hole Museum. They took offence at the museum dressing up dead gophers for the entertainment of unethical people. It was probably around the same time as I last raised PETA's ire for questioning their intelligence for sending a six-foot talking carrot to the hinterland where it stood outside schools trying to convince beef farmers' kids to become vegetarians.

The owners of the Gopher Hole Museum took PETA's criticism in stride. They went right out and got three more dead gophers stuffed to depict the story of the ruckus. A museum curator gopher is playing tug of war with a member of G.A.G.S. (Gophers Against Getting Stuffed). The rope in the tug of war is the third dead gopher.

As if the displays weren't enough to fill my head with wonder, I couldn't have possibly been prepared for the museum's own song. I've heard country songs about trains, pick-up trucks, dogs, and cheating wives, but this was certainly a first – a song about a room full of stuffed, dead, gopher carcasses. I won't subject you to the lyrics, which go on (and on, and on, and on) for six long verses.

I'm not completely sure, but I could have sworn that as I left the museum, somewhere in the distance banjo strings were being plucked carrying the theme song to the movie Deliverance across the flat (except for those three hills) prairie.

Well... I Think It's An Emergency

I've often thought that the whole 911 emergency call system is inadequate. Oh sure, the people who answer the calls do a great job sending the fire department or the paramedics out to assist you, but there are so many more things that they could be doing to serve their communities. Perhaps what we need is a full range of three-digit calling codes to help us get through the other emergencies of day-to-day life.

Naturally, I have a few suggestions.

Dial 211 for missing recipes.

Last Thanksgiving we were faced with a major culinary crisis. The scrap of paper that my mother's pumpkin pie recipe was written on thirty years ago had disappeared. It's a well-known fact that one cannot celebrate Thanksgiving without pumpkin pie. It may even be against the law in certain parts of the country. It would have been so much easier if we could have just picked up the telephone, dialed 211, and had someone either tell us where we had last put the recipe or tell us just how much nutmeg my mother used in her recipe. Without that service we were forced to spend hours tearing apart the kitchen in search of that scrap of paper.

Dial 311 for English to teenager translation services.

Now that my sons are in their twenties, we seem to be able to communicate a whole lot easier. It wasn't quite so easy during those turbulent years between 1993 and 2001 when we cohabitated with teenagers. A three-digit emergency calling number would have been invaluable for parents like us who had difficulty understanding the meaning of typical teenage terminology.

I'm sure my wife and I are not the only parents who have had difficulty understanding that when a teenager says, "OK" it doesn't necessarily mean agreement with whatever you are asking him to do. That simple "OK" could mean anything from, "I'm saying 'OK' just to get you off my back and I'll forget whatever it is you are asking by the time you leave my room," to "If I say 'OK' to anything you ask now, I'll get to watch that vein pop up on your forehead later when you discover that I didn't really mean I agreed to do it."

Dial 511 for television mediation services.

It was hard enough when the boys lived at home to get control of the television. It seemed that whenever there was something I wanted to watch there was a rerun of the Simpsons that they needed to see, just in case they had missed some of the intellectual nuances the first twelve times they had seen that episode. Now that there is just my wife and I vying for control of the remote, I am just as likely to end up watching a rerun of Star Trek when I would prefer to watch ESPN. A quick dial television mediation service might give me a fighting chance to catch a few minutes of a hockey game during the commercials.

Dial 611 for computer explanations.

I don't ask a lot from my computer. I expect it to turn on when I push the button, and I think it's pretty reasonable that it stay on until I am finished working. I realize that that probably sounds pretty naïve to anyone who has even the slightest understanding of how computers work.

When I worked in large corporate setting I had staff that always seemed to take a coffee break just at the exact moment when I needed their attention. Apparently my computer has pretty much the same attitude. Whenever I really need it to do something it will make the monitor screen turn blue, tell me push CTRL-ALT-DEL, and forget everything I have typed during the previous four hours. When that happens I should be able to pick up the phone, punch three numbers and be connected to someone who can explain in simple English why that happens. Even if they can't explain why it happens, they could try to talk me out of jumping out my office window when it does.

Dial 711 for retaliation.

I'm sure I'm not alone when I say I would like to be able to punch in three digits on my telephone the next time a telephone solicitor calls me at dinner time. The person at the 711 call center could take the details of my retaliation emergency and respond by calling the telephone solicitor back at 3:00 AM every night for a month.

It's clear that these additional emergency call services are needed because the people at 911 get pretty cranky when I call them with a missing pumpkin pie recipe report.

At The Sound Of The Tone It will Be Exactly Sometime Or Another

It never ceases to amaze me that there are so many people who have no concept of time. I'm not talking about the perpetually late or the terminally tardy. That can usually be blamed on any number of things ranging from dysfunctional alarm clocks to not giving a darn about the people who are waiting around for your arrival. The time-maladjusted people that I am referring to are the ones who think that, if it's 11:00 where they are, it must be 11:00 where everyone else is in the world too.

There are four main time zones across the continent. Five if you add in the Canadian Atlantic Provinces and six if you take in the extra half hour that Newfoundland tacks on just to be different. Most of the population deals with the first four. Calling Newfoundland can be an adventure because you always have to wonder if the guy holding the tin can will be able to pull the string tight enough for your call to get across the Gulf of St. Lawrence.

Living on the West Coast means we get started on our day well after the people in the East. There seems to be no end to the people who feel that they want to call me from Toronto, New York, or Penobscot at 8:00 in the morning. What they don't seem to realize is that in my world it's only 5:00 AM.

To make matters worse, I am not what you would call a morning person. My communication skills don't usually kick in until a couple of hours after my eyes are open. My eyes are rarely open at 5:00 AM. My brain is closed then too. There are days when it doesn't open for business at all, but I'm sure that's not a big surprise for most of you.

When I get a 5:00 AM call, my end of the conversation is usually limited to, "Hug glow... Huh... Wittiest... Obey"

I received one of those calls this morning. It was deeply disturbing because my wife is currently about 3000 miles away and she would surely know that when she isn't around I am probably going to sleep a bit longer than usual.

It wasn't her.

It was for her.

The caller desperately needed to get in touch with her. He was from the car rental agency that she had dealt with back there. Rather than wait the few hours until she was due to return the car, he thought it might be a good idea to call here to see if she had suddenly decided to drive all the way across the continent before driving all the way back to return the car.

Apparently the last person who rented the vehicle wanted to know if they had left something in the car when they returned it. Even now, when I am fully awake, I'm not sure how I was supposed to know.

My son, who had also picked up the phone, was able to provide me with the details. He was surprised that, even though I was clearly not very awake, I was able to give the person a fairly detailed answer that included speculation on his intelligence quotient, the marital status of his parents, and the current location of his head, which would have required a nimbleness on his part that would exceed that of a Cirque due Solely performer.

I must admit that I have, on occasion, made use of the reverse effect of the time shift between the West Coast and the East. I have been known to call my brother after midnight on New Year's Eve when it was after 3:00 AM for him. I don't think I ever tried it on my sister though, because every younger brother in the world knows that older sisters are much more creative than brothers when it comes to retaliation.

The temporally confused can even be located in the same time zone. I have a person who calls me on occasion from California, who always needs to ask what time it is here. I've tried explaining that we are in the same time zone, but he just can't quite get it. If Florida is three hours different from LA, then Vancouver, a city almost as far away can't possibly be at the same time as him. I've finally given up trying to convince him. If he asks me my time when it's 3:35 PM on a Wednesday, I give him the only answer that seems to satisfy him.

"Right now it's exactly 10:17 AM last Monday."

Cow-erring Under A Heat Wave

The people who live on the Pacific Coast north of California tend to be a rather temperate bunch. That has nothing to do with our alcohol consumption. It's a reflection of the climate in the region. We like it temperate, not too hot, and not too cold. If it goes above 75 degrees Fahrenheit (24 degrees Celsius for my metric readers) we are sweltering. If it drops below 50 degrees Fahrenheit (10 Celsius) we start preparing for the next ice age.

A few days ago the temperature soared to 102 Fahrenheit (39 Celsius) in my little town. I hid inside all day. I fully expected to see Satan sitting on one of my deck chairs saying, "Well, at least it's a dry heat."

My wife, on the other hand wasn't quite as lucky. One of her side projects that she works on all year is our local community day, which includes a parade, a barbecue, and fireworks. Diane was responsible for the parade judging. Luckily the parade was in the morning when the temperature hadn't peaked. Even so it was still hotter than anything we had experienced in several years. Her biggest concern was avoiding the little puddles of melted humanity that seemed to be everywhere along the parade route.

Temperatures like that might be commonplace in places like Arizona, but something is terribly wrong with the planet when it starts to get that hot in my backyard. A few days later the answer crossed my desk in the form of a news item that many of you might have missed. Scientists have determined that global warming is being accelerated because of cow breath.

Ken Olsen, a range livestock nutritionist at Utah State University said, "Most people want to talk about belching and farting, but that's just a small percentage of the gas released by cows."

Mr. Olsen might want to talk about cows belching and farting, but I for one would just as soon be a long way away when they do it. In fact I'm surprised that someone from Utah would even say the word "farting' because that is the only state that one of my books wasn't stocked by bookstores because it had the word 'peed' in its title.

He went on to say that 90% of the methane produced in cows' stomachs is absorbed into their bloodstreams and exhaled through the lungs, leaving just 10% for the aforementioned belching and farting. Researchers believe that the methane is of no benefit to the cows and in fact producing it wastes up to 16% of the energy provided by their feed. Having spent a reasonable amount of time in barns, I can assure you that the methane is also of no benefit to anyone who has to go anywhere near the south side of a cow when it's facing north.

Thank goodness we have scientists to help us with problems like this. A research team from the University of Nebraska is trying to develop an additive for cattle feed that will cut down or eliminate the methane cows exhale. It's obvious from the news item I read that they really know what they are talking about.

Dr. Stephen Ragsdale, the lead researcher wasn't afraid to use extremely technical language when talking about this topic. I try to avoid being so technical in my writing, but I think it's important that my readers hear what he had to say so that they can understand the problems of cow breath too.

He said, and I am quoting directly here to avoid any confusion, "Cows are big animals."

I probably don't need to tell you that you could have knocked me over with a feather with that revelation.

Another scientist wanted to put all of this into perspective. He pointed out that the agriculture sector only produces 5% of the greenhouse gasses that are causing global warming, while other industries produce 35%. What has me worried is his statement that 31% of these gasses are produced by 'personal emissions.' That raises a whole batch of questions, most notably, how do they measure someone's personal emissions.

I'd hate to think where the gauge goes.

It also makes me wonder if the heat wave that struck here might have been entirely my fault. I did have a couple of chilidogs the night before, and we all know what they can do to your personal emissions.

Googling Yourself Can Be Fatal

The English language is changing at a pace so rapid; many of us just can't keep up. One of the more disturbing trends in recent years is the creation of new verbs from nouns. People no longer meet. They conference. It brings up the question of, do you go to a conference to meet people, or do you hold a meeting to conference with someone?

Don't worry. It confuses me too.

Someone recently asked me if I wanted to get together and "starbuck." At first I thought it was an obscene proposal, but apparently I was just being invited for a cup of coffee. I'm not sure if I was relieved or disappointed.

Eventually it becomes easier to just accept the new verbs and incorporate them into your vocabulary. Failure to do so will probably make it difficult to do a crossword puzzle in the not too distant future. I tried out one of the new verbs just the other day.

I googled myself.

When someone suggested I try doing it I had some concerns. Frankly, it sounded like something that might make hair grow on the palms of my hands or make me go blind if I found that I liked it and googled too often.

Googling is not nearly as bad as it sounds. Google™ is one of the main search engines on the Internet. Therefore to google someone is to look them up using Google™. Self-googling is a perfectly permissible, although perhaps a bit narcissistic, pastime.

I learned a lot about myself while googling. Some of it I was pretty sure about before, but there were some oddities.

It was a little spooky to discover that I am buried in a cemetery near Grant, Alabama. It's one thing to discover that you might be dead, but it's entirely another matter do discover that you might be dead AND in Alabama.

Apparently there is a football stadium named in my honor at Catawba College in North Carolina, where once again I am dead, this time since 1953 at the age of 48. All along I thought I was born in 1953. It's nice to know though that I was so well thought of before my birth that I have been named to several sports halls of fame, albeit posthumously.

People have often asked me about my apparent leadership in the field of small mammals, particularly shrews. When people search for books I've written in online bookstores they often are astounded to discover that Gordon Kirkland is also the author of *Advances in the Study of Peromyscus (Rodentia).* It turns out that Gordon Kirkland has also left this world; this time at the age of 51.

I was beginning to get a bit concerned about the early deaths of Gordon Kirkland. Thankfully I found that I had also recently died at the age of 91 in Pennsylvania. Boy; that was a relief. In reading my obituary I discovered that if I am the small mammal expert, then I was also my own father... or perhaps I am my own son... or... OK, now it's just giving me a headache.

You can imagine my surprise when I discovered that I was one half of the US Men's 40+ Doubles Racquetball Championship team in 2002. I always thought that racquetball was one of those games that take a lot of running around to play; something my spinal injury makes me somewhat deficient at. I think it would be very hard to play racquetball with Tara my assistance dog at my side. She'd be torn between her job of keeping me standing and her inbred canine desire to chase the ball.

Even when I was in the kind of physical condition needed to play games like racquetball I avoided them like the plague. I tried squash once and came to the distinct conclusion that the game got its name from the effect of a rubber ball traveling at supersonic speed hitting that part of the anatomy that you would least like to have injured in such a way. I walked funny for a week and discovered that I could reach higher notes than Frankie Valli did when he sang Sherry Baby with The Four Seasons.

Strangely enough, it turns out that Gordon Kirkland is also the president of a company that makes special equipment for airplanes in, of all places, Kirkland, Washington.

I don't even like flying.

...and if it keeps killing me, I don't think I'm going to enjoy googling myself all that much either.

I'm Not Distracted...Oooooh!
The Ace of Spades

It's been a couple of years since I've written about the ever-increasing problem of distractions facing the drivers on our roads.

In my father's day the most noticeable distraction was the truck drivers who seemed to insist on blaring their horns at him for no apparent reason. What wasn't all that noticeable was that I was looking out the back window and pumping my arm every time a trucker got behind us. More often than not, the truckers would oblige me and give a good hard yank on the lanyard that operated their air horns.

The sound of the horn would always be followed by the sound of my father saying, "What in the name of Pete...!!!"

I never knew who Pete was, but I think of him whenever I hear a trucker blare his horn.

I gave up that practice after we nearly hit the ditch one hot summer day. That was the day that I reached the pinnacle of scaring the crap out of my father behind the wheel. When a trucker blew his horn Dad was just raising an ice cream cone to his lips. Its route could later be tracked by the path of ice cream up Dad's right cheek ending where he inserted it into his ear. I really impressed myself with that one. I just knew I could never surpass it no matter what. There was no point even trying.

Today's drive is full of distractions. Other drivers are probably the biggest distraction around. It's really annoying that you have to take your mind from important things like answering the telephone, sending a text message on your handheld computer, and reading a novel just to keep an eye on how bad the other drivers are. I saw a driver this morning with a cup of coffee in one hand, his telephone in the other, and a date book propped against his steering wheel. I don't even want to think about what he might have been using to steer.

Billboards have become a major distraction lately. A billboard can't just be a sign for one product anymore. Now they have to change every few seconds. I've seen drivers slow down so that they can get a good look at every ad.

I find it particularly distracting when they do that. How I am I supposed to keep my train of thought on the telephone conversation I'm having, the words to the song on the radio AND look out for drivers who want to see what's on sale at Wal-Mart this week?

Adding DVD players and Video screens to cars just seems a bit too weird for me, and frankly, my weirdness tolerance is pretty darn high. The guy who hit my car thirteen years ago had been looking for a cassette tape on the floor of his car instead of paying attention to the fact that traffic had stopped ahead of him. Now I'm going to be living in fear of someone watching Julia Roberts' rear end instead of mine.

My car has its share of distracting gadgets. I have my CD player, my tape deck, my telephone, and my wife. At any given point any one of these can be distracting. I even find the gas gauge quite distracting these days. I'm still trying to figure out how my gas tank expanded to the point where it now holds $48.00 worth of gas.

When I first got the car I had trouble putting $20.00 worth in it.

I've just discovered that I have a computer in my car. I think the same people who wrote the Windows software might have programmed it. Every time I wanted the car to do something simple like move forward, it shut itself off. My mechanic determined that the onboard computer was the culprit and it needed to be replaced.

He and I have a symbiotic relationship. I depend on him to do anything more complicated than refueling, and he depends on me to send him to Hawaii every winter. If Jeff says my car has an $852.11 computer, and it needs to be replaced than I just go along with it. If he said the car needed to have its onboard passenger-side banana replaced, I'd probably go along with that too.

It's probably for the best that I forget there is a computer in the car. If I could ever figure out how to play solitaire on it, I'd be almost as distracted behind the wheel as I usually am at my desk.

Is It Real, Or Is It Mesmerizing

I've been watching a lot of TV lately, and I have to say this whole "Reality TV" thing confuses me. I have a question that no one seems able to answer:

Whose reality are they supposed to be about?

We've been inundated with shows about people pretending to be millionaires, men looking for the perfect trophy wife, women looking for the perfect man, and castaways on vacation in places that anyone with half a brain would avoid like the plague.

OK folks, hands up anyone who has every done anything like what is portrayed on these shows. I have eaten some strange things in my life. I have even had a few hair-raising experiences, but nothing I have ever done or eaten comes close to what I see on TV's version of reality. You won't find me swinging from any construction cranes and following it up with a hearty meal of insects and animal reproductive organs.

I guess I have a certain prejudice against these shows. As a writer I have to object to any form of television that doesn't employ writers. There are no scripts for these shows, most likely because none of the participants could remember their lines if there were. I'm sure two thirds of the writers in Los Angeles who are not too busy clearing tables in restaurants and driving taxies, are trying to find some way of cashing in the phenomenon.

If nothing else they can try developing concepts for the next great "reality" show. Since I've always been a firm believer in the concept of if you can't beat 'em, join 'em, I think I'll put a couple of proposals forward. For example:

Beer Factor

Contestants are transported to an uninhabited island in Lake Erie. They are provided with an unlimited supply of beer but no other food or drink. During the 7 weeks of show production the contestants must participate in a number of skill testing competitions such as, shaving after a breakfast of 12 premium imported bottles of beer, bobbing for Budweiser®, and counting to ten.

Survivor - East Texas

Twelve participants are given French Peugeot cars to drive through East Texas. Each car will be adorned with bumper stickers saying, "I am a French U.N. Delegate," "I'd rather Veto you than surrender to Germany... Again," and "Make Wine Not Beer." Drivers will race through East Texas with the objective of actually surviving. No one will be "voted off the island." The final winner will be the one who successfully makes it out of the area alive. If no participants make it to the finish line, the one who traveled the furthest will be posthumously declared the winner and will receive the funeral of his or her dreams.

Joe Bachelor

By combining two recent concepts, we could have the perfect reality show. One man will pretend to be unmarried in a chalet full of women trying to win him for themselves. After narrowing down the field each week to a final two candidates, Joe Bachelor will finally admit that he is actually married with a family of four, but he hopes they can all still be friends.

American Idle

Forget the talent search. Forget the judges and critics. American Idle will focus on a group of unemployed men and women who have no desire to seek jobs. They will somehow be able to afford alcohol, cigarettes, and other recreational consumables and they will interact with the show's gun-toting regulars.

Some stations may continue to air this show under its original title, Cops.

Of course we are all sitting mesmerized by the latest reality show to hit the airwaves. In a classic cost saving measure, every TV network in the United States and Canada is airing the same show – Survivor: Baghdad Bunker.

While some of the other survivor series have participants that the audience hopes will go on to win the game, this show is filled with unpopular characters. We aren't quite sure about who may have already been voted out of the bunker, but we remain ever hopeful that the show will have its final episode soon. No one wants to see it renewed for another season. Unfortunately it's the only one that can claim to be giving its audience a dose of reality in every broadcast.

There is one piece of reality that all of these shows reinforce with every episode. It's the reality that we've all witnessed ever since the first fuzzy black and white pictures were broadcast into our living rooms:

Imitation is the sincerest form of television.

I Have Memories I Can't Forget And Some I Can't Remember

One of the great mysteries of the human brain is the problem we have getting things to stop repeating inside our heads. Think about it. If someone mentions Gilligan's Island to you, your mind will immediately start replaying the theme song. Odds are it will still be repeating it four or five hours later.

My mother was always quite amazed that I could recite the words to the Oscar Meyer Weiner Song, but couldn't remember where I had left my shoes. Today my wife wonders why I can remember the Bugs Bunny theme song, but I can't seem to remember where we keep the laundry basket.

I can erase useless data from my computer. In fact with my degree of computer literacy I can also remove important data pretty easily. Why can't I send things to the wastebasket of my mind and keep them there?

When my sons were young we were told that it was important to read to them, even beginning before their vocabularies went much beyond goo and gaa. We bought dozens of books ranging from Disney classics to Doctor Seuss. As the boys grew, they became attached to a few of these stories and bedtime wouldn't go ahead as planned without reading one of the favorites. As a result, twenty years later, I can still recite Yurtle The Turtle.

"On the faraway Island of Salamasond, Yurtle The Turtle was king of the pond. A nice little pond, it was clean, it was neat. The water was warm there was plenty to eat...."

My sons were hooked on TV shows like Sesame Street and Mr. Rogers when they were little. I can still hear the themes to both of those programs inside my head. Mr. Rogers may be gone, but 'It's A Beautiful Day In The Neighborhood' will probably stay in my mind for the rest of my life. I have always considered myself most fortunate because my sons were born early enough that the annoying purple dinosaur didn't invade our house.

I still can't escape the latest in children's television and their mind numbing songs. Each morning when I watch the morning news, a commercial encouraging me to come to see a live show by someone called Bob The Builder interrupts the latest information coming from the news centers of Baghdad, Washington, and Moose Jaw, Saskatchewan. Clearly, by the look of the characters in this show and the ages of the people in the audience, Bob The Builder must be the latest in a long line of children's programming.

Don't get me wrong. I'm all in favor of the educational elements of these shows. Children know more about their world, the alphabet and numbers at a far younger age than we ever did. My problem is with the theme song. Hours after the rest of the commercial has faded from memory, I still have "Bob The Builder... Yes We Can" repeating in my head like a broken record.

I might only see a commercial featuring a hot supermodel or a great looking car once during the news. Good old Bob The Builder shows up every half hour without fail. To make matters worse, they have used the half-length commercials that appear at the beginning of a commercial break and again at the end. 'Bob The Builder... Yes We Can' is reinforced so that I have no choice but to go about my business mentally singing along. Three or four hours later I am still hearing it.

Again, and again, and again....

Hopefully when the Bob The Builder live show moves on to another city it's theme will recede into the back of my mind. It had better. I have so many more important things that I need to remember every day.

I need to have instant access to the part of my memory that lets me know when the next hockey game is going to be telecast. I need to remember when my column deadline comes around each week. I need to remember how to tie a Windsor knot.

And of course, above all, I need to remember that, "The turtles were happy. Quite happy indeed, until Yurtle The Turtle, the king of them all, decided the kingdom he ruled was too small..."

When My Mind Wanders It Brings Back Souvenirs

It's no secret that my mind tends to wander. In fact, it wanders so much that I almost expect it to come back someday wearing a t-shirt that says "I went to Nantucket and all I got was this stupid t-shirt."

Not only does my mind wander, but it wonders an awful lot too. I'm never too sure whether it has wandered because it was wondering or if it wondered because it was wandering. I wonder about a lot of things that the average person would never think of thinking about.

I wonder why I do that.

I know that I am not alone in this state of wondering and/or wandering. During the SARS outbreak my brother wondered if it is safe to go to Toronto as long as you wear a coffee filter over your face. It turned out that it was, but only if you weren't going to be in contact with anyone exposed to SARS.

I once heard comedian Billy Connolly raise the question, "When man discovered that he could get milk from a cow, what was he thinking he was doing at the time?"

That's the very sort of thing that gets my mind wandering and wondering.

For example, when the first escargot was eaten, was it on a prehistoric dare? Eating a snail is not something that is overly high on my personal to do list. Did two early Frenchmen sit around in their caves trying to fight the boredom of surrendering themselves to being eaten by a German saber-toothed tiger, when a snail came into view?

Did one say, "Hey, Pierre, I triple dog dare you to eat that snail."

Did the other say, "Mais oui, Jean-Guy, even though you jumped all the way to the triple dog dare, which, even in our prehistoric times, is a severe lapse in etiquette, I will eat that snail, but could I put some garlic butter on it first?"

The darer probably said, "You could, but we haven't invented garlic butter yet."

Current affairs can also jumpstart my wandering/wondering mind. I've been wondering lately if the owner of that restaurant in Baghdad that was bombed shortly after Saddam and his sons entered had the forethought to get them to pay their bill in advance.

With Canada decriminalizing marijuana, will that change the meaning of "This bud's for you?"

Can you treat mad cows with anger management therapy?

Can veterinarians treat the Dixie Chicks for foot in mouth disease?

Of course television can get my mind packing for a long trip. I was wondering the other day if you lose your case on a TV courtroom show on channel 22, could you appeal to a higher court on channel 47?

I wonder what will happen to Jerry Springer once he's had every redneck in the country on his show. On a related wonder, will the supply of rednecks for Jerry Springer keep increasing at the same rate as his show's guest total adds up?

Why don't government regulatory bodies improve the intelligence level of television by banning small business owners from making their own commercials?

While I wouldn't willingly sit through an hour of the latest iteration of Survivor, it wouldn't make me start thinking about throwing a brick through the screen. In my viewing area, I am subjected to commercials for car dealerships, carpet salesmen, and furniture stores that leave me looking for the nearest available concrete block.

One flooring retailer dresses up in regal robes and puts a crown on his Yorkshire Terrier and announces that he has decreed the lowest prices in all the land.

The dog looks slightly more intelligent than his owner, and stares out at the viewers with a look that seems to be saying, "For the love of Pete, please, somebody, call the SPCA..."

A local car dealer takes cruelty a step further by putting his children in his commercials. Those kids are probably afraid to show their faces at school. Child welfare agencies could probably prevent a lot of random acts of wedgies by saving children from entrepreneurial parents who make them go on TV and say things like, "My daddy's low, low prices can put your daddy in a new car, even if the banks have turned him down for a loan."

Another burning question knots up my shorts every time I go to the bank machine. If banks make such huge profits from the service charges that they put on everything from cashing a money order to providing pens that actually have ink in them for you to fill out your deposit slips, why can't they make the glue on the envelopes at the instant teller machines taste better?

I think that's a pretty important question. We deserve an answer. Let's face it, anyone who has ever had to lick a bank deposit envelope knows that it leaves you feeling like something crawled into your mouth and died. You'd think that they could take a few dollars from the gazillions of our dollars sitting in their coffers and spend it on some flavoring for the envelopes. I think cherry might be nice. Imagine how much nicer it would make you feel about turning over your hard earned paycheck to cover the overdraft in your bank account, if licking the envelope gave your mouth a minty freshness, instead of an image of the horse that gave its life for that glue.

Since my mind had wandered that far from what I was doing I decided to call the customer service line at my bank and ask them why they are too cheap to make their envelopes taste better. I don't think the woman who answered the call was quite prepared for the question. It was met with several seconds of dead silence.

Finally she managed to say, "I beg your pardon, sir...?"

"Envelope glue," I said. "Paying my credit card bill leaves enough of a bad taste in my mouth without adding to it with envelope glue that tastes like something the dog did on the carpet. I'd like you to get better tasting envelopes, please."

More silence.

"I don't think I can help you," she said.

I'm not sure but I am almost positive I heard her say under her breath, "Perhaps psychiatric care might do you some good."

I try not to let my mind wander when I am driving, but at times it disobeys my orders and takes an entirely different route home. Some of my road wonders include:

Would calling in a cruise missile strike against the motor home doing half the speed limit in the passing lane really be considered an excessive use of force?

Does your insurance cover dry cleaning if a bird craps on you when you are driving a convertible?

Shouldn't people in SUV's have to drive along the median or off to the side of the road to show that they really need 4-wheel drive?

If you put one of those "Jesus is my co-pilot" bumper stickers on your car, does that allow you to drive in the car pool lane? Obviously the woman I saw doing just that the other day thought so. You'd have to think though, if Jesus really was her co-pilot, he'd tell to do the speed limit.

Home life brings about its own special sorts of wonders and wanders. I regularly wonder how a loaf of bread that is whole at 11:00 PM can be reduced to a couple of crusts by 6:00 AM, and then I remember that my son has moved back home.

I wonder why, if two people both snore, only the male can be criticized for it. Even after thirty years of marriage, I still wonder if the day will ever come when I can be right about something and still not end up being wrong.

Of course all of this mind wandering and wondering could just be a symptom of my incredibly short attention sp...

Oooooh. There's a flock of geese outside my window.

About the Author

Gordon Kirkland is one of North America's premier humorists. His syndicated column, Gordon Kirkland at Large, first appeared on August 27, 1994, and has been running in Canadian and American newspapers ever since.

His first book, Justice Is Blind – And Her Dog Just Peed In My Cornflakes, won Canada's Stephen Leacock Award of Merit for Humour in 2000. His second book, Never Stand Behind A Loaded Horse drew critical acclaim with reviewers' comments such as, "nothing is sacred with someone who has no qualms about turning any situation into a fantastically funny event!"

Gordon has entertained audiences at live appearances and on radio and television shows. In 2004 he was named to the faculty of the Erma Bombeck Writer's Workshop.

Printed in the United States
35499LVS00005B/88-1110

9 781420 811490